KNOWING
GOD'S WILL

Also available in the "How To" series:

Effective Evangelism	Ben Davies
Enjoying God's Grace	Terry Virgo
Growing Up as a Christian	Roger Day
Handling Your Money	John Houghton
Joining the Church	Richard Haydon-Knowell
Leading a Housegroup	Richard Haydon-Knowell
Learning to Worship	Phil Rogers
Praying the Lord's Prayer	Terry Virgo
Presenting Jesus in the Open Air	Mike Sprenger

For further information on the "How To" series and New Frontiers International, please write to New Frontiers International, 21-23 Clarendon Villas, Hove, Brighton, East Sussex, BN3 3RE.

SERIES EDITOR
TERRY VIRGO

How to...
STUDY SERIES

KNOWING GOD'S WILL

PHIL ROGERS

NEW FRONTIERS INTERNATIONAL

WORD PUBLISHING

WORD (UK) Ltd
Milton Keynes, England

WORD AUSTRALIA
Kilsyth, Victoria, Australia

WORD COMMUNICATIONS LTD
Vancouver, B.C., Canada

STRUIK CHRISTIAN BOOKS (PTY) LTD
Maitland, South Africa

ALBY COMMERCIAL ENTERPRISES PTE LTD
Balmoral Road, Singapore

CHRISTIAN MARKETING NEW ZEALAND LTD
Havelock North, New Zealand

JENSCO LTD
Hong Kong

SALVATION BOOK CENTRE
Malaysia

KNOWING GOD'S WILL

© Phil Rogers 1990.
Published by Word (UK) Ltd/New Frontiers.

All rights reserved. No part of this publication may be reproduced or transmitted in any form or by any means, electronic or mechanical, including photocopy, recording, or any information storage or retrieval system, without permission in writing from the publisher.

ISBN 0-85009-185-3 (Australia 1-86258-092-8)

Unless otherwise indicated, Scripture quotations are from the New International Version (NIV).
© 1978 New York International Bible Society.

Other Scripture quotations are from the following sources: The New American Standard Bible, © 1960, 1962, 1963, 1968, 1971, 1972, 1973, 1975, 1977 The Lockman Foundation (NASB).
The Authorised Version of the Bible (AV).
The Amplified Bible, © 1962, 1964, 1965, 1977, 1986 The Zondervan Corporation and the Lockman Foundation.

Typeset by Suripace, Milton Keynes and printed and bound in Great Britain by Cox & Wyman Ltd., Reading.

FOREWORD

The 'How to' series has been published with a definite purpose in view. It provides a set of workbooks suitable either for housegroups or individuals who want to study a particular Bible theme in a practical way. The goal is not simply to look up verses and fill in blank spaces on the page, but to fill in gaps in our lives and so increase our fruitfulness and our knowledge of God.

Peter wrote his letters to 'stimulate wholesome thinking' (2 Peter 3:1). He required his readers to think as well as read! We hope the training manual approach of this book will have the same effect. *Stop*, *think*, *apply* and *act* are key words.

If you are using the book on your own, we suggest you work through the chapters systematically, Bible at your side and pen in hand. If you are doing it as a group activity, it is probably best to do all the initial reading and task work before the group sessions – this gives more time for discussion in key issues which may be raised.

Most quotations from the Bible are from the New International Version, which the reader is expected to use in filling in the study material. Where other versions are used, this is indicated in the text.

Terry Virgo
Series Editor

NEW FRONTIERS INTERNATIONAL is a team ministry led by Terry Virgo and involved in planting and equipping churches according to New Testament principles with a view to reaching this generation with the gospel of the Kingdom. They are also responsible for a wide range of conferences, training programmes and the production of printed and audio teaching materials.

Contents

Introduction	The Problems of Guidance	9
Chapter 1	The Will of God	14
Chapter 2	The Knowledge of His Will	19
Chapter 3	The Perfect Plan	25
Chapter 4	If the Lord Wills	30
Chapter 5	The Way of Wisdom	35
Chapter 6	Praying for Guidance	40
Chapter 7	Hearing God's Voice	46
Chapter 8	Signs and Wonders	52
Chapter 9	Taking Counsel	58
Chapter 10	Many Counsellors	65
Chapter 11	Vocation and Marriage	71
Chapter 12	Church	79
Chapter 13	Ministry and Home	85
Chapter 14	Making the Final Decision	92

Introduction THE PROBLEMS OF GUIDANCE

If there is one question that concerns a Christian more than any other, it is: "What is God's will for my life?" Much time is taken up in prayer and in counselling, seeking to know the will of God. But frequently we come away confused and uncertain. Why does it often seem so hard to know what God wants for us?

There are times when the Lord guides us with such clarity, yet at other times we pray and pray and heaven seems to be as brass! There are some people we meet, and authors whose books we read, who always seem to be so clearly directed by the Spirit and frequently use such phrases as, "The Lord said to me...", "The Lord told me to do..." But do we hear the Lord's voice in the way they seem to? Why aren't we confident enough to use such phrases ourselves? There are those occasions, however, when we feel really convinced that this is something God has told us to do and yet the consequences are disastrous. Why is guidance so difficult?

The aim of this study is to show that much of the difficulty we have about guidance is because we often approach it in entirely the wrong way. In order to see clearly what the scriptures do teach on the will of God and guidance, we will need to highlight these mistaken preconceptions. For the popular view on divine guidance, despite its wide consensus amongst Christians, does not stand up to Biblical scrutiny. So let us begin by looking at some typical assumptions and briefly evaluating them.

Guidance - A Popular View
- God has a specific individual will for my life which is His perfect plan for me.
- Each of us is required to discover what that specific will is.
- We do so by seeking God in prayer and by reading the signposts.

- The signposts (sometimes called the harbour lights) are:
  1. the scriptures
  2. our circumstances
  3. the inner witness of the Holy Spirit.
- We make our decisions on the basis of the agreement of these signposts and we know that something is the will of God when all three agree. Just as a boat can sail safely into harbour only when all three harbour lights are lined up, so we can safely proceed with a matter *only* when we are sure that the scriptures, circumstances and our inner peace concur.

This is a simple, straightforward approach. It is popular and frequently seems to work. Yet it raises a number of serious issues. Here are a few of them.

1. If it is our responsibility to discover our own personal perfect plan, we will be bound to make mistakes at times and get it wrong. There may even be occasions when we deliberately choose to take certain actions *we* want to take despite knowing them deep down to be wrong. In either situation we "miss God's perfect plan". So, intentionally or accidentally, we find ourselves doing something not according to God's plan, and this is described as living in "God's second best". Is there such a thing? Is that really a Biblical concept?

    Consider this situation. A young man falls for an attractive lady in his church. Their relationship becomes quite physical rather too quickly – they seek counsel and are advised to make sure it really is God's will for them to marry. However, the pressure of desire precipitates them into a quick wedding and the young man suppresses some of his inner feelings of misgiving. After they wed, they begin to face difficulties. The man begins to review their courtship: "Was it really God's will? Have I actually missed God's perfect plan and now got stuck with this difficult woman for life? If only I had taken the trouble to discover God's will." Then along comes another young lady; she seems to be everything his wife is not. He thinks, "Not so attractive, but what a lovely person she is. She would make the perfect wife. But we are Christians and God's word forbids divorce, so I've got to stick it out till death us do part. I'll just have to put up with *God's second best*. If only I had waited for God's perfect plan and not been in such a hurry." The other young lady is soon snapped up by another eligible bachelor. In our husband's view of the whole situation, she was God's perfect plan but through his own stupidity he missed it and ended up with God's second best!

Clearly such an interpretation of events and such an attitude to life is appalling, not just unbiblical. This is the kind of extreme situation that can arise out of this popular view of guidance.

2. In order to live comfortably with the popular view it is necessary to split life into two distinct areas. One is that routine part of life where we make our own decisions and do not seek guidance, feeling that it would not seem right to ask, "Lord, what would you have me do?" in matters so trivial. God's will or principles of guidance are not really relevant to the 'everyday decisions' we make all the time. It is only when we move into the second area of 'big decisions' that we have to seek God's will and try to discover it by reading the signposts.

This is actually quite inconsistent. Why should the 'perfect plan' only involve major decisions and not minor areas? Is not the God who upholds the whole universe also the One who knows the hairs on our head and indeed upholds every molecule and atom? How do we determine which decisions need guidance and which ones do not?

Some dear saints seek to avoid this inconsistency by trying to live like Jesus, who "only did what He saw His Father doing." Expecting constant impressions from above concerning even the minutest detail of life, they pray for guidance as to which brand of baked beans they should select from the supermarket shelves and deduce that God is saying, "Take the proprietary brand, not the named brand", because they watch three people before them each take the shop's brand and ignore the other. This must be the Lord's direction.

While this appears absurd in this instance, what about a big decision like buying a car? A Christian might pray, "Lord, we need a new car. Please guide me to the car of your choice, your perfect plan for our transport at this time." Prayer time over, he switches on breakfast T.V. and, lo and behold, an advert for the Cavalier. Later he picks up the free newspaper from the front door mat, casually opens it and suddenly his eye catches a page full of Vauxhall Cavaliers for sale. On his way to the station he counts no less than fifteen Cavaliers that pass him. "Two or three witnesses." (See 2 Cor 13:1.) He tells a Christian friend later, "The Lord has clearly guided us to go for a Cavalier this time."

A Biblical understanding of guidance will lead us to a consistent practice of decision-making without leading us into such absurdities.

3. If we believe that God has a plan, yet it is up to us to discover it then we are involved in something like a spiritual treasure hunt. If finding God's will is seen as a matter of reading the signposts and interpreting the clues, then we are just participators in something like a vast cosmic game that God is playing with us, giving us the clues to see if we are clever enough to figure it out. And if we do not figure it out, and therefore make a wrong turning, what then? Do we get another go? Can we miss God's perfect will, or does He always overrule? And if God always overrules, then what is the point of trying to discover His will in the first place? If it is all going to work out according to His sovereign overruling plan anyway, we need not bother to seek guidance or waste all the time and emotional energy it takes to try and find out what He wants.

There are a number of other issues we could have raised which will be covered in this study, such as 'words from God', 'the place of prophecy' and 'counselling'. These are so easily misused with the traditional approach. To say, "God told me", gives decisions an incontravertible sense of authority that silences any further comment or counsel, usually unhelpfully so!

Does God have a perfect plan for each one of us that we are personally responsible for discovering? What does the Bible say? It is amazing how certain verses of scripture seem to reinforce the popular view when read with this assumption. We read a verse such as Romans 12:2 – "Then you will be able to test and approve what God's will is..." – and immediately assume that by "God's will" Paul is referring to this perfect plan. But is he?

We need to lay aside such assumptions and approach the text afresh, so that we can see what the Bible actually says and not what it seems to say in the light of preconceived ideas of guidance. So before we move into the first study chapter, let us pray.

Father, thank You for Your Word, the Bible, which corrects and teaches us so that we may be completely equipped for every good work. Please help us to clear our minds as we look into Your Word. We ask for Your precious Holy Spirit to lead us into the truth and give us the revelation You have promised us, for Jesus' sake. Amen.

Chapter 1   THE WILL OF GOD

What is the *will of God*? There are actually several places in the scriptures where the will of God is specifically defined for us, so this is not a difficult question to answer. Look up the following references and write them out.

God's Will Defined

1 Thess 4:3 *It is God's will that you should be sanctified: that you should avoid sexual immorality;*

1 Thess 5:16-18 *Be joyful always; pray continually; give thanks in all circumstances, for this is God's will for you in CJ.*

1 Peter 2:15 *For it is God's will that by doing good you should silence the ignorant talk of foolish men.*

These probably seem strange definitions of God's will to us. Read over the passages above several times and try to summarise what they teach about the will of God.

be sanctified;
happy & prayful
doing good;

You will have noted that God's major concern is with our *character*, *responses* and *behaviour*. Moral purity, right attitudes and responses, and righteousness in all our dealings are the scope of these passages. We might summarise them all with the text, from 1 Peter 1:15-16, "But just as he who called you is holy, so be holy in all you do: for it is written: 'Be holy, because I am holy.' " God's will is our *sanctification*. That means living moral lives, characterised by prayerfulness, thanksgiving and joy, that challenge the sinful and selfish attitudes and behaviour of the non-Christian environment in which we live.

So then, the will of God is firstly *our sanctification*.

A Second Definition
However, this must be seen in the broader context of God's will for us. Here is another definition. Write out John 6:40:

For my Father's will is that everyone who looks to the Son and believes in him shall have eternal life.

We might summarise this text thus: "God's will is our *salvation*". It was to accomplish God's will to save us that Jesus came into the world. He came to do the will of God. How are we to understand that? Look up and write out the following verses:

John 4:34 *"My food", said Jesus, "is to do the will of him who sent me and to finish his work.*

John 5:30 *By myself I can do nothing; I judge only as I hear, & my judgement is just, for I seek not to please myself but him who sent me.*

John 6:38 *For I have come, not to do my will but to do the will of him who sent me.*

It is clear from these passages that the will of God that Jesus came to do was to fully accomplish our salvation, so that He would not lose a single one of those the Father gave to Him, but would raise every one up on the last day. This is salvation in its entirety. For us today it means past, present and future salvation, which clearly involves us living a life of obedience and holiness, being strong to the end and obtaining the goal of our faith, the salvation of our souls (Matt 24:13, 1 Pet 1:9). By working out our salvation in this way we are doing the will of God, just as Jesus did the will of His Father by living a life of obedience – even to the point of death on the cross for *our* salvation. Read over Matthew 1:21, Acts 2:23 and

Philippians 2:6-8. What predetermined plan did the Father have for Jesus' life?
That he would die on the cross for his peoples' sins.

Write out Hebrews 10:10. Jesus came to do His Father's will, "and *by that will, we have been made holy through the sacrifice of the body of JC once for all*."

Hence we see that God's declared will is our *salvation* and *sanctification* so that (Heb 10:36) *You need to persevere so that when you have done the will of God, you will recieve what he has promised.*

God's Will for Me

While this may seem a rather broad and vague concept of God's will, it is essential that we understand that this is God's specific will for each one of us personally and individually. The NASB translation of James 1:18 (first half) reads, "In the exercise of his will he brought us forth by the word of truth". How does the NIV translate it?
He chose to give us birth through the word of truth.

When God chose us, He exercised *His will*. He chose the twelve apostles (John 15:16) and the Apostle Paul (Acts 22:14), and He has also chosen and willed to save each one of us. Read Ephesians 1:4-11.

When did He choose us? (v.4)
before the creation of the world.

Why did he choose us? (v.4)
To be holy and blameless in his sight.

16

Here it comes again – "holy and blameless" – God's will is our sanctification.

To what has He predestined us according to His will? (v.5)
to be his sons through JC

How does Paul, at the end of verse 10, define the mystery of His will that He has made known to us?
to bring all things ... together under one head even christ.

It's no secret

God does have a great universal plan that He works out according to His will. In it, you and I have been specifically and individually included. However, I cannot infer that 'the mystery of His will for my life' is a hidden, specific personal plan for me individually, which I have to discover. Notice the mystery of His will has already been made known to us. The secret is out! God's will for my life has already been made known, and that is my total *salvation* and *sanctification*.

Therefore, God's will for my life is not something hard to find, something hidden, enigmatic, secret and mysterious. It is something plainly defined in the scriptures, that we can all clearly state. *This* is God's will for my life – *is my salvation + sanctification*

Review the scripture passages we have looked at and expand on this key definition of God's will.

....
....
....
....
....

Back to the Bible

It was quite a surprise to me when I realised what the Bible actually meant by the term '*will of God*'. It is easy for us to take a word or phrase to mean something it does not really mean and thus to misread the scriptures. The 'fleshpots' of Egypt had nothing to do with sexual appetites; 'adoption' is not the same as our modern day practice; and 'will of God' does not refer to 'the option God wants us to choose' whenever we have to make a non-moral decision. Yet this is so often what we read into texts such as the second part of Romans 12:2 – "Then you will be able to test and approve what God's will is – his good, pleasing and perfect will." We think automatically in terms of 'right decisions' instead of what it really means, 'godly behaviour'.

When Jesus taught us to pray "Thy will be done", He did *not* mean, "May we always choose the right option, the one You intend us to take, in every decision we make." Rather, He meant, "May we always live as You desire us to live in holiness and godliness." It has to do with our character, conduct and conversation rather than plans, decisions and right choices; what we are and how we behave rather than what we do.

| THE WILL OF GOD IS THE WAY GOD WANTS US TO LIVE. |

Can we miss the will of God? Yes: whenever we *sin*. All sin is outside the will of God. The root meaning of the word 'sin' is to miss the mark. When we sin we miss the target, we break God's law, we act in unbelief, we fail to do His will and we displease Him. God has no second best. He has a best and a worst: the best is to live in the obedience of faith, the worst is to sin.

Write out James 4:17:

Anyone, then, who knows the good he ought to do and doesn't do it, sins.

As we go on to consider the matters of guidance and decision-making, it is essential that we first lay this foundation. We need to see where God's priorities lie and make sure we only use the phrase 'will of God' in a Biblical way.

Chapter 2 THE KNOWLEDGE OF HIS WILL

As we read the New Testament epistles in particular we see how essential it is that we *know* the will of God. Look up the following passages and write out the verses in the space below:

Acts 22:14 Then he said: 'The God of our fathers has chosen you to know his will and to see the Righteous One & to hear words from his mouth.

Romans 12:2 Do not conform any longer to the pattern of this world, but be transformed by the renewing of your mind. Then you will be able to test & approve what God's will is — his good...will

Ephesians 5:17
Therefore do not be foolish, but understand what the Lord's will is.

Colossians 1:9 For this reason, since the day we heard about you we have not stopped praying and asking God to fill you with the knowledge of his will through all spiritual wisdom and understanding.

In this last verse Paul does not use the common word for 'knowledge' here. Paul wrote this letter against the backdrop of false teaching. Certain teachers (called Gnostics) claimed that they had special knowledge

(Gnosis), that they were 'in the know' in a way that those who did not share their 'spiritual experience' could not possibly be. "We have seen", "God has told us" was the way they spoke. Paul attacks this super-spiritual heresy by praying that everyone might be filled with "the knowledge of his will". The word he uses for 'knowledge' means to ascertain, perceive and recognise in a clear way. It is like getting to know someone you already know more fully. It is like going back to somewhere you have visited before – it all comes back to you, but then there is more to discover that you had not noticed before.

So, knowing God's will is so important, not just in the broad sense that we defined in the last chapter, but by becoming familiar with all its particulars. We already know and recognise the will of God, but we need to be *filled* with the recognition of it. Just as He chose Paul to know His will, so He has chosen each one of us that we might fully know it. So how do we get to know it?

David Knew All God's Will

Let us look at an Old Testament man of God.

What does it say of David in Acts 13:22? He was *a man after God's own heart, he did everything I want him to do.*

How did he know all God's will in order to carry it out? Psalm 16:7 speaks of God counselling David, especially at night – but what was the basis of that nocturnal instruction? Psalm 1:2:

meditated on God's Law.

Find Psalm 40:8. Write out the first half:

I desire to do your will, O my God;

The second half tells us why:

your law is within my heart.

This is the key to David's ability to do all God's will. Here we see how David's will became conformed to the Lord's will. He came to delight to do it as he meditated on God's word.

Write out Psalm 37:31:

The law of his God is in his heart his feet do not slip.

Psalm 119 is, of course, the classic passage on this subject and perhaps the best-known statement in this whole Psalm is verse 105. Write it out:

Your word is a lamp to my feet & a light for my path.

Now let us turn to the New Testament.

Read Romans 2:18. How can we know God's will?

Be instructed by the Law.

'The law' referred to in this verse does not mean a set of God-given rules and regulations to be learned and adhered to. The law is something delightful, to be loved and treasured above all other possessions. It is the expression of God's heart of love towards His creation. It is the will of God which we obey for our own safety and blessing, since it brings us the joy and delight of righteousness and frees us from the shame and regret of unrighteousness. The Jews of Jesus' time spoke of the whole Old Testament as 'the Law and the Prophets' but today we can think of the whole of the Bible as 'the law of God' in the sense that David uses this term in the Psalms.

Read Hebrews 8:8-12 and write out the relevant sentence in verse 10:

I will put my laws in their minds and write them on their hearts.

This is something that God does whereby our will and God's become one. Our desires become God's desires. And so we come, like David, to know all God's will, not in our heads in a legalistic way but in our hearts by the grace of God.

Write out Psalm 37:4:

Delight yourself in the LORD and he will give you the desires of your heart.

The Will and the Word of God
Clearly then our knowledge of God's will depends on our knowledge of scriptures, for

> TO KNOW THE WILL OF GOD IS TO KNOW THE WORD OF GOD.

Look back at Romans 12:2 that you wrote out at the beginning of this chapter. What is the renewing of our mind? It is clearing our minds of man's nonsense and filling it with God's wonderful truth. We can only renew our minds by feeding upon the scriptures and this has the wonderful effect of *transforming* us. Note it is *transformation* and not *information* that we are after, and that comes from meditating and feeding on the Word and not just reading it. What is the outcome of such mental replenishment? (Rom 12:2)

being able to test and approve what God's will is - his good, pleasing and perfect will

Paul speaks of us testing God's will. The proof of the pudding is in the eating, and the proof that God's will is good, acceptable and perfect is seen as we renew our thinking by conforming it to His revealed Word, and see the outcome in transformed attitudes and behaviour, and the effect these have on our lives.

The will of God is not a 'secret to be discovered' for it has been clearly revealed to us in the scriptures. Here we find everything that God wants laid out for us.

In the scriptures we see:
- God's character and attitudes
- conduct that pleases Him (and also that which does not)
- the passions and concerns of God's heart for the world
- God's plans and purposes for His Church.

Through the scriptures we gain:
- the knowledge of the nature of life
- insight and understanding of the issues that face us
- wisdom that enables us to choose and act rightly.

Read again 2 Timothy 3:14-17. Write out verse 17 in the space.

God has given the Scriptures *so that the servant of God may be thoroughly equipped for every good work.*

Underline the words 'thoroughly' and 'every'.

There are no short cuts. The only way to know the will of God is to soak ourselves in the Word of God; to fill our minds, meditate and indeed gorge ourselves on His wonderful book and let God write it into our very hearts.

The Spirit and the Word

Now what about the Holy Spirit? We read that the Holy Spirit "will guide" us "into all truth" (John 16:13), and that Jesus was "led by the Spirit" (Luke 4:1). Also, the anointing of the Spirit teaches us all things so that we do not need any person to teach us (1 John 2:27). Some have taken these passages to imply that the Spirit gives us such immediate revelation of truth that we do not need to read the Bible. Such teaching has been popular in recent years – quiet times, Bible reading and expository preaching have been ridiculed. It has been said that the Bible is not a textbook but a test-book to confirm the truth the Spirit is teaching us in our hearts as we cultivate a relationship with Him.

This is a false dichotomy. How does the Spirit lead and teach us? He takes the very words that He originally inspired to be written down and brings them to life for us, writing them upon our hearts (Heb 8:10). The Holy Spirit teaches us all things on the basis of the Word He has already spoken.

Copy out John 14:26: *But the Counsellor, the H/S whom the Father will send in my name, will teach you all things and ill remind you of everything I have said to you.*

The Spirit reminded the disciples of Jesus' words. So too He reminds us of what we read in the scriptures. Certainly we do not want some self-sufficient dry Bible knowledge, but neither do we want the opposite extreme, seeking to live solely by voices from heaven or inner impressions attributed to the Holy Spirit, without any reference to scripture. If we only read the Bible we will 'dry up'. If we only listen to the Spirit we will 'blow up'. But if we listen to the Spirit as we read the Bible, we will 'grow up' and be filled with the knowledge of His will.

> *Lord, I live by Your word,*
> *Lord, I live by every word from Your mouth,*
> *And I'm like a tree by a stream,*
> *I'm bearing fruit, my leaf is green,*
> *All that I do is prospering, O Lord,*
> *I live by Your word.*
>
> *As the rain and the snow come down from heaven,*
> *And water the earth, and bring forth its fruit,*
> *So shall be the word that You are speaking,*
> *It shall not return empty to You,*
> *It shall accomplish Your desire*
> *It will surely succeed,*
> *Your word transforms the desert,*
> *And Your word is changing me.*

Mark Altrogge.
Copyright © People of Destiny International/Thankyou Music 1984.

Does your heart echo David's words, "I desire to do your will, O my God" (Ps 40:8)? "Yes, Lord, I really want to do Your will and to please you." Then give yourself more fully to feasting on the scriptures, letting the Holy Spirit engrave them ever more deeply upon the tablets of your heart.

Chapter 3   THE PERFECT PLAN

In seeking to answer from the Bible the vexed question, "What is God's will for my life?", we have discovered so far that God's will is plainly revealed to us and that it relates to our *conversion,* our *character* and our *conduct.* God's will is our salvation and our sanctification, and the fine detail of it is found in the scriptures. The more we dig into God's Word and invite the Holy Spirit to write it into our hearts, the more we will be filled with the knowledge of His will. But the difficulties we face over guidance have more to do with decision-making than conduct. When we ask, "What is God's will?" we are usually asking, "What option does God want me to choose?" rather than, "How should I behave or react?" What does the Bible say about God's will concerning our non-moral decisions?

As we saw in the first chapter, the popular view of guidance is based on the assumption that God has a specific will for each individual person, a perfect plan or ideal blueprint for each person's life. Consequently, the individual's responsibility is both to discover what that plan is and then, in obedience, to work it out. But does the Bible really teach such a notion? Does the Lord have our whole lives mapped out for us?

The Life of Joseph

When we consider the lives of men and women of faith as described in the Bible, we find clear evidence that God has specific plans and intentions for certain individual lives. Perhaps one of the most spectacular examples is that of Joseph.

Early in his life, God gave him two dreams predicting the future, which were fulfilled through an extraordinary sequence of events. What was Joseph's perspective on the events of his life? Write out Genesis 50:20:

You intended to harm me, but God intended

it for good to accomplish what is now being done, the saving of many lives

Notice that his testimony is one of hindsight. He looked back and saw God's hand in the strange events of his life. He looked back and saw how his early dreams had been fulfilled. If you are familiar with the story, proceed with the following statements, writing TRUE or FALSE alongside each one. If not, first read Genesis chapters 37-50.

TRUE/FALSE

a) Joseph received dreams after praying for guidance from the Lord. ......FALSE......

b) Joseph's dreams came to him sovereignly from God without solicitation. ......TRUE......

c) These dreams were promises that he could do nothing about. ......TRUE......

d) They guided him as to what action he should take. ......FALSE......

e) At each major crisis, Joseph sought God's will and acted on the answer. ......FALSE......

f) At each crisis, Joseph found himself in situations beyond his control. ......TRUE......

g) Joseph got very insecure about what was happening and moaned to God. ......FALSE......

h) He rested secure in the knowledge that he was in God's hands and got on with life in a godly and righteous way, making the best of his situation. ......TRUE......

i) Joseph continually worried about whether he was doing God's will and was always trying to get a word from God to know what to do. ......FALSE......

j) Joseph knew that God was with him and he got on with doing whatever presented itself, confidently trusting in the Lord. ......TRUE......

God had certain specific *purposes* for Joseph's life, purposes which were fulfilled quite apart from any decision-making on Joseph's part. We see this again and again in the lives of Biblical characters. When action was required, God initiated it by giving a command and the man of faith obeyed. Sometimes in fear and doubt they argued back, as did Moses and Gideon, but the Lord always won the argument and His words were obeyed.

The Sovereignty of God

There is a delightful verse in Psalm 115:3. Write it out: *pleases Him / Our God is in heaven, he does whatever*

God is King over all the earth (Ps 47). But he is no constitutional monarch. He *actually* rules over and determines everything that happens, as King Nebuchadnezzar discovered. Write out his testimony from Daniel 4:35:

All the peoples of the earth are regarded as nothing. He does as he pleases with the powers of heaven... No one can say to him: "What have you done?"

The Psalms are full of glorious statements that declare God's kingly rule. We call this the *sovereignty of God*. Write out Psalm 33:10-11:

The LORD foils the plans of the nations; he thwarts the purposes of the peoples. But the plans of the LORD stand firm forever, the purposes of his heart through all generations.

God has plans for nations. We can see this in the whole history of Israel. Read through Jeremiah 29:4-14, and then write out verse 11:

"For I know the plans I have for you" declares the LORD, "plans to prosper you and not to harm you, plans to give you hope and a future."

God's plan for Israel involved exile in Babylon. For Joseph it included slavery in Egypt. For Jesus the predetermined plan was death on a cross (Acts 2:23, 4:28). This plan is not some ideal blueprint in which everything works out pleasantly and prosperously. This plan involved times of great difficulties and tribulation but God's overall purpose was blessing. Write out the well-known statement of Paul in Romans 8:28:

And we know that in all things God works for the good of those who love him, who have been called according to his purpose.

Each one of us has a part to play in God's eternal purposes. This is so eloquently declared in David's Psalm 139. Read verses 1-16. What do you think is meant by the last three lines of verse 16?

The length of his life.

Before we move on to look at the way we should respond to God's sovereignty, let us examine its parameters. What is its scope? We have already seen from Psalm 139 that it includes:
- details of our birth
- the length of our life.

Look up the following references and write out the areas in which God's purposes are declared in each verse.
- Eph 1:5... *be adopted*
- Acts 13:48... *to have eternal life*
- Acts 13:2... *for the work God had called them to*
- Rom 12:3,6... *act sober by faith, gifts according to faith*
- 1 Cor 12:11, Heb 2:4... *work of the Spirit, gifts of the spirit*
- First verse of 1 Cor, 2 Cor, Eph, Col & 2 Tim... *called to be an apostle.*
- Eph 2:10... *good works*
- 1 Cor 7:7,17 & Matt 19:11-12... *gifts and life*

Clearly God has a predetermined plan for the whole universe, and our own individual lives feature within that plan. This is God's sovereign will and it seems to focus particularly on our becoming a Christian and the subsequent role He has chosen for us as part of His Church.

There is, however, no suggestion that we have to discover this plan. It is God's plan and the initiative is totally and always His. Most of the time, like Joseph, we only see how God has worked in our lives *in retrospect*. We can look back on life's ups and downs and see the way God has led us. Frequently God's purposes unfold through events over which we have no control, yet which change our lives. Sometimes God breaks in with specific supernatural instructions to be obeyed, usually when we least expect them. If we are to understand the principles of guidance and know how to make right decisions, it is essential that we have an awesome appreciation of God's utter sovereignty and bow before His irresistible power!

Write out Romans 9:19-20:

One of you will say to me; "Then why does God still blame us? For who resists his will?" But who are you, O man, to talk back to God? "Shall what is formed say to him who formed it, 'Why did you make me like this?'"

Chapter 4 IF THE LORD WILLS

Clearly God has an eternal sovereign purpose that embraces our own individual lives; however, that remains His business and not ours. He only tells us what He chooses to tell us and that is always at His initiative. Our responsibility with respect to this plan is not to try and discover it – but to live our lives with the sense of security and trust that comes from *knowing* that He works it all together for good. That does not mean everything that happens will be good any more than Joseph's experiences were good, or the agony of Christ on the cross was good. In the end, however, we *do* see the good, as did Jesus, "who for the joy set before him, endured the cross, scorning its shame" (Hebrews 12:2).

Read 1 Peter 4:12-19, James 1:2-3, Matthew 5:11-12. Summarise in your own words what attitude and response we can have to trials and troubles.

Rejoice & be glad, trust that God knows what's happening, persevere.

There is undoubtedly a mystery concerning the interplay between God's purposes and Satan's right to test us. Read Job chapters 1 and 2, also Luke 22:31-32, John 10:28-29, 1 Corinthians 10:13. What can we conclude about our security in the face of Satan's right to demand permission to test us?

We will not be tempted beyond what we can bear and our salvation is secure because God is faithful.

What important statement about God did Paul make in 1 Corinthians 10:13 that we need to hold on to at all times?

God is faithful.

If God is sovereign and He allows evil things to happen, does that not make Him evil? No, because the Bible shows us that man is fully responsible for his own sinful actions. In Acts 2:23 we read that, according to God's pre-determined plan, Jesus was nailed to the cross by the hands of godless men. Read the verse carefully. If it was God's plan, does that relieve those men of their responsibility for their actions? ~~YES~~ / NO.

Turn to Acts 4:27-28. Write out verse 28:

They did what your power and will had decided beforehand should happen.

Did that exonerate Herod, Pilate or the Gentiles?   ~~YES~~ / NO

Does this make God the originator of evil?   ~~YES~~ / NO

Read Matthew 26:24, Luke 22:22 and John 6:70-71. Jesus' betrayal was predicted, and He knew from an early stage that Judas would fulfil that prediction. Clearly the passage indicates that it was foreordained and yet at the same time Judas is totally responsible. In God's perspective these are not irreconcilable. This is a paradox and some Bible teachers reject it as they do not like and will not accept such logical tensions. But we cannot tie up all the ends. God's Word declares God's absolute sovereignty and man's total responsibility, so we must hold them both. As it says in Isaiah 55:8-9, God's thoughts and ways are superior to ours.

God's sovereign will is supreme, yet we cannot say, "God made me do it." Man is a free moral agent and totally responsible for every decision he makes, yet in retrospect we see how God has been at work in the events of our lives. Paul puts it succinctly in Philippians 2:12-13. Write out verse 13 :

for it is God who works in you to will & to act according to his good purpose.

31

What we work out, God works in. We decide, but God *wills*. We take action, but God works in us according to His purpose. Solomon sums it up in Proverbs 16:9. Write it out:

In his heart a man plans his course, but the LORD determines his steps.

See also verses 1, 4 and 33.

So there is no ideal blueprint to be discovered. Life is for living with its blessings and its troubles, knowing that God is with us and at work in us. Paul puts all the difficulties of life on this earth into the right perspective in 2 Corinthians 4:16-18. Read these verses and write out verse 17:

For our light and momentary troubles are achieving for us an eternal glory that far outweighs them all.

We see that God's ultimate purpose is not bound up in the transient blessings and problems of our homes, families, jobs or church, but is eternal and will be realised on that day when Jesus raises us up with Him on the last day.

The Backdrop
Therefore we live our lives against the backdrop of God's *sovereignty and faithfulness*. We rest in the knowledge that the Lord is King and works all things according to the purpose of His will. We live also against the backdrop of *eternity*, that this world is not home, but we are strangers and sojourners just passing through. We rest in the knowledge that whatever life brings, there is laid up for us hereafter a crown of righteousness, which the Lord will award to us on that glorious day of His appearing.

How are we to live life against this backdrop? A very significant passage is found in James 4:13-17. Write out verse 15:

Instead you ought to say, "If it is the Lord's will, we will live and do this or that."

Is it wrong to make plans?..... *No*

What is James telling us about our attitude to decision-making?

Our decisions must be influenced by God's will

Here is a classic statement concerning decision-making against the backdrop of God's sovereignty. Look up these other examples and write out the particular phrase about God's will used by the writer.

1 Peter 3:17 ..... *if it is God's will*

1 Corinthians 4:19 ..... *If the Lord is willing*

Acts 18:21 ..... *If it is God's will*

Acts 21:14 ..... *The Lord's will be done*

Turn also to Romans 15:30-32.

What is Paul urging them to do? ..... *to pray*

What for? (v. 31) ..... *His rescue and recapture in Jerusalem*

Why? (v.32) ..... *so that by God's will he might have joy and be refreshed*

Is he saying, "Pray that you may know what is
'God's will' for me"?   YES / ~~NO~~

Is he saying, "I already know it is 'God's will'
for me to come to you"?   ~~YES~~ / NO

As you can see, the phrase "by God's will" is equivalent to those written above. It is the same as saying, "If the Lord wills", and shows us how Paul acknowledges the backdrop of God's sovereignty. He is actually not in the least concerned as to 'what the will of God is' nor 'whether it is God's will or not', because he has no concept whatsoever of 'God's perfect plan for his life', consisting of a detailed blueprint to be discovered and followed. Paul lived in the hands of the One who rules and overrules all things; who arrested him on the Damascus road and sent him out as an apostle. He lived, with an all-consuming awareness of God's eternal purposes, so that by all means he might save some.

If the Lord Wills

Although this expression is very Biblical, many of us have had a reaction against the use of such a phrase, especially in prayer. Too often it has been the practice of Christians to hedge their bets by qualifying every prayer with "if it be Thy will". This kind of apologetic, uncertain praying, devoid of any real conviction and faith, is rightly banished from our prayer meetings. Any perspective of God's sovereignty that robs us of passion, conviction or determination is distorted. It smacks more of Islam than of Biblical Christianity. The 'will of Allah', that leads to resignation, apathy and indolence, is the very opposite of what we are speaking of here.

Listen to Paul's words in 1 Corinthians 4:18-19. "Some of you have become arrogant, as if I were not coming to you. But I will come very soon, if the Lord is willing, and then I will find out not only how these arrogant people are talking, but what power they have." You can imagine them getting the letter – "Please Lord, don't let him come soon!"

Paul deals with their arrogance and boasting firmly but without arrogance and boasting himself. "If the Lord wills" is an expression of dependence upon and submission to the Lord. More than anything else it is an attitude of having everything in the right perspective.

James certainly does not mean us to lace every prayer with "if the Lord wills" or qualify all our plans with "D.V." (Deo Volente, Latin for God willing). He means us to have an attitude and awareness of our total dependence upon God. Our God is in heaven, He does what He pleases, and we are totally secure in His almighty hands.

Chapter 5 THE WAY OF WISDOM

In Ephesians 5:17 Paul writes, "Do not be foolish, but understand what the Lord's will is."

Now we might have expected him to say, "Don't be foolish but be *wise*", but here we see that the opposite of being foolish is understanding what the Lord's will is. This *is* wisdom. Thus we can make this definition:

WISDOM IS TO UNDERSTAND WHAT THE LORD'S WILL IS.

We have already looked at Colossians 1:9 where Paul asks God to fill the Christians at Colosse with the knowledge of His will. How does he complete the verse? *all spiritual wisdom and understanding*

Wisdom may be defined as "applied knowledge" or "know-how" – as the dictionary says, "the ability to make the right use of knowledge". Wisdom is to knowledge what technology is to science. It is knowledge put to use. It is not enough to know what is right, to know the will of God. We need *understanding* and *insight* into the ways of God – so that we know *how to apply* our knowledge, and put it to use in all the decisions we have to make in life. In everything we need wisdom to make right decisions – from the most trivial decisions as to what brand of beans to buy at the supermarket to the monumental life-changing decisions we all have to make from time to time. There is only *one* way to make all our decisions, *one* way of making right choices, and that is *the way of wisdom*.

Turn to Proverbs chapter 4, read the whole chapter and summarise verses 5 to 9 in your own words: *Wisdom is so important that you must do all you can to get it because it will be a good protection*

Copy out verse 11:

I guide you in the way of wisdom and lead you along straight paths

If an earthly father seeks to guide his son in the way of wisdom, how much more will our heavenly Father? *God guides us in the way of wisdom.* To understand this is to know what divine guidance really is, and know how to make right decisions.

The book of Proverbs is jam-packed with wisdom. Rather than take up pages and pages of this study looking at these important statements, may I recommend a recipe to increase wisdom. Proverbs has 31 chapters and there are seven months – January, March, May, July, August, October and December – which have 31 days. Do you want wisdom? Read one chapter of Proverbs per day during those seven months. Seven times through the book in one year will give you great wisdom, insight and understanding. On the alternate months choose other parts of the Bible to read. If you are already well-versed in the scriptures, choose one month every year to go through Proverbs.

The Wisdom of God
As you read about wisdom, of whom does it remind you? Read Proverbs 8:22-36.
Who does that sound like? *Christ*
Turn to 1 Corinthians 1:24. Who is the Wisdom of God? *Christ*
What does Paul tell us in Colossians 2:3?

that Christ has all the treasures of wisdom and knowledge.

Not only is Jesus Christ the embodiment of God's wisdom, but Paul tells us in 1 Corinthians 1: 30 (NASB), "by His doing you are in Christ Jesus, who became to us wisdom from God, and righteousness and sanctification and redemption". What a salvation we have in Christ! How we rejoice that He has made us righteous and redeemed and sanctified us! But do we also rejoice that He makes us *wise*? Have we seen that our salvation is essentially being made wise? He has delivered us from *foolishness* and brought us into *wisdom*. Copy 1 Corinthians 1:30 from the NIV:

It is because of him that you are in Christ Jesus, who has become for us wisdom from God — that is, our righteousness, holiness and redemption.

The whole section from 1:18 to the end of chapter 2 is very important. Here we see human wisdom, the way that seems right to man, contrasted with God's wisdom, which seems stupid to man's natural thinking. In Christ, we who were once stupid have now been made wise. Once we could not accept the truth, but the Holy Spirit opened our eyes to see what we hitherto could not see and to believe what we hitherto would not believe. We saw our own foolishness and through Christ we received the wisdom of God. The cross made sense. We could now appreciate God's astonishing plan of salvation. In Christ we began to see everything from a whole new perspective – we began to gain insight into life such as we had never imagined before. We began to understand what God had freely given to us in His amazing grace. Paul concludes chapter 2 with a very important statement. Write out the last sentence of verse 16:

But we have the mind of Christ.

He is saying this of the 'spiritual man' (v.15) which is not some supersaint, but the ordinary Christian who is in Christ and has received the Holy Spirit from God (v.12), and who, with a teachable heart, eagerly absorbs words taught by the Spirit.

The Spirit of Wisdom
When we are filled or baptised with the Holy Spirit we receive the same Spirit who rested upon Christ. Write out Isaiah 11:2: *The Spirit of the LORD will rest on him — the Spirit of wisdom & of understanding, the Spirit of counsel & of power, the Spirit of knowledge & the fear of the LORD.*

Write out Ephesians 1:17:
I keep asking that the God of our Lord J.C.

the glorious Father may give you the Spirit of wisdom and revelation, so that you may know him better

In this prayer Paul is not asking God to give the Christians at Ephesus something they do not have, for clearly they have already received the Spirit (v.13), but he is asking for more of His wisdom, that they might be strengthened (see Eph 3:16). Even when we have received the Spirit of wisdom, we need more wisdom, ever-increasing wisdom. We need to go on being filled with the Spirit of wisdom. Let us make this our daily prayer.

So then we see that, having become Christians, we now walk in the *way of wisdom*. Just as Jesus knew His Father's heart and was able to make wise decisions, so we have the mind of Christ. The Holy Spirit within us gives us the very same wisdom and insight and understanding, so that we too can confidently make decisions that are wise and right. It is essential then that we know that Christ has made us *competent to make right choices*.

Whatever Your Hand Finds To Do
One of my favourite verses in the scriptures is Ecclesiastes 9:10. Read from verse 7 and then copy out verse 10:

Whatever your hand finds to do, do it with all your might, for in the grave, where you are going, there is neither working nor planning, no knowledge nor wisdom

Life is so short and we won't be making plans when we're dead, so let's make our plans with wisdom *now* and execute them with all the energy and enthusiasm that God gives us. That is precisely how the apostle Paul lived his life and fulfilled the work to which the Holy Spirit called him (Acts 13:2,4). In fact, the book of Acts is excellent for gaining insight into how God guides. With 28 chapters it is worth reading a chapter per day, one month each year, when you are not reading Proverbs. In it we see instances of sovereign, supernatural intervention and direction, but most of the time we see Paul moving on from place to place, sometimes just passing through, sometimes staying longer, responding to each situation as it opened up to his ministry. Paul's guidance was often "let's do this" (e.g. Acts 15:36) or "it seemed good" (e.g. Acts 15:22 NASB).

Read the opening verses of Luke's Gospel. How did Luke get his guidance to write this God-breathed part of the scriptures? (v.3):

It seemed good also to me

What a staggering statement for a task of such profound significance! But that is precisely how God's eternal purposes are generally accomplished: by godly men and women doing what seems good to them, doing it with all their might, and diligently employing all their skills and gifts in accomplishing their plans.

Notice how Luke first weighs it all up. Having carefully investigated everything, it seemed good. This is the way of wisdom. It is not impulsive. It is not presumptuous. It makes and executes plans with a deep sense of dependence upon God and a recognition of the backdrop of His sovereignty.

Fear of the Lord
Write out the first part of Proverbs 9:10:

The fear of the LORD is the beginning of wisdom

This is essential if we are to walk in the way of wisdom. This is not just a passive acknowledgement of God's sovereignty. Unless the axe is laid to the roots, we will always face pressure in our lives. We must come to the place of giving ourselves unreservedly over to God, having died to self-interest. Only then will we be able to walk in the way of wisdom and know the guidance of God. If we allow other attachments to interfere with our availability to God, putting other things first before God's kingdom and His righteousness, we will make foolish decisions not pleasing to God.

What does the Lord require of us? Copy out the answer from Micah 6:8: *To act justly and to love mercy and to walk humbly with your God.*

This is the way of wisdom. If we walk in it, we will be what we are made to be, live as we have been called to live, and do what we really want to do from the depths of the new heart God has put within us.

Chapter 6 PRAYING FOR GUIDANCE

If we are competent to make our own wise decisions, how does prayer fit into the picture? If God sovereignly rules over our lives and it is not up to us to discover His plans for us, how should we pray when we have decisions to make? The popular view, described in the introduction, encourages us constantly to seek the Lord in prayer in order to know what He wants us to do, whereas the 'way of wisdom' appears to make decision-making an impersonal process, and to undermine our prayer life.

Read James 1:5-8. In many of the straightforward decisions of life, God has already given us all the wisdom we need. We know exactly what to do, how to act, what choices to make, and we can do so without specifically asking God for wisdom. However, that does *not* mean that we exclude God from such situations. Remember, God's will for us is that we *pray continually* (1 Thess 5:17). If we already know what to do then we ask God in prayer to help us accomplish it.

Look again at James 1:5. If anyone lacks wisdom, what should he do?
ask God for it.

What two things does James tell us here about God?
1. *he gives generously* 2. *without finding fault*

The NASB translates the latter "without reproaching". In other words, He does not tell us off, saying, "Why are you bothering me? Haven't I given you the mind of Christ and the Bible? Go away and work it out for yourself." No, the Lord does not reproach us, rather He delights in our dependence and trust. "Lord, help! I need your wisdom!" What promise does James make?
and it will be given to him.

Isn't that great! Write it out again in capital letters!

IT WILL BE GIVEN TO HIM.

However, as Christians we often find ourselves getting very confused when seeking guidance. When 'trying to find God's will' in a situation, we often fall into the very double-mindedness described in verses 6-8. We pray, "Lord, what should I do? Do *you* want me to take this option or the alternative? Which is the *right* one? Lord, I'm so confused. Please tell me what to do."

All sorts of thoughts go rushing round our heads and we try to clear our minds so we can hear from God. We desperately want a word from heaven, but when thoughts pop into our minds we do not know if they are from God or just our own thoughts. So we rise from our knees still confused and postpone our decision because "we haven't heard from God yet." We feel tossed backwards and forwards. We can't make up our minds and our indecision makes us unhappy, perhaps even irritable, grumpy and 'down'. What does James write in verse 8?

he is a double minded man, unstable in all he does

God has not called us to be double-minded and unstable.
He has called us to clear thinking and confidence. Uncertainty, indecision and unbelief are not meant to be the characteristics of God's children, *yet so often they are!* What are we to do?

Repent of unbelief and pray for wisdom with the expectation that if we ask of God, He will give it to us.

Jesus Prays Before A Major Decision

Read Luke 6:12-13. Here is Luke's account of how Jesus prayed before choosing the twelve apostles, who were to be the foundation of the Church. It was a decision of enormous significance.

Now this is how the account is often understood, in the light of popular assumptions:

> Jesus went out to spend the whole night in prayer in order to be quite sure He had discerned His Father's will on the matter. He sought God and waited upon Him throughout the night until eventually the Father fully revealed to Him the names of the twelve.

The lesson we learn from this is: If we want to know God's will then we have to wait on God until we are absolutely sure we have heard from Him, even if it takes all night!

But who actually chose the twelve, Jesus Himself or the Father? Look at John 6:70, 13:18, 15:16,19. What is common to all these verses?

.....Jesus chose them..

Turn to Mark 3:13-14. According to Mark, on what basis did Jesus choose the twelve?

.....they were the ones he wanted...

If Jesus had to pray all night in order to wrest some names out of His Father, does this give the impression of One who gives generously without reproach?   **YES** / NO

Guidance is not heavenly hide-and-seek. God does not reward us with the answer only when we score enough points or clock up sufficient prayer time. Jesus did not pray in order to elicit twelve names from His Father because *He already knew who He wanted*. He knew it was His responsibility to choose the twelve and He had already done so.

So what *did* He pray? He would certainly have asked for wisdom, and also consulted His Father about each of those He was considering. But when Jesus prayed, *HE PRAYED!* He poured out His heart in earnest entreaty for those twelve men, passionately expressing His hopes and desires for each of them and for the Church of which they would be the foundation stones. When Jesus prayed it was to secure God's blessing upon the twelve men He had chosen.

Prayer is ... Praying!

Prayer is essentially asking God to act. In prayer man comes before almighty God with his humble requests. In prayer we express our wishes, hopes and desires before the presence of the One who alone can do something about them. We pray *in order to be heard by God*. Throughout the Old Testament men cry, "Hear us, O Lord", "Hear from heaven", "Hear my cry, O Lord." Write out the relevant lines from the following Psalms:

4:1 .....hear my prayer...

17:1 *Hear O LORD my righteous plea, Give ear to my prayer*
27:7 *Hear my voice when I call*
28:2 *Hear my cry for mercy*
65:2 *O you who hear prayer*

This is the character of God. See also Matt 6:7, Luke 1:13, John 9:31.
Complete the following in your own words:
God is one who *listens to our prayers*

We also pray *in order that God may give us what we ask.* Even before we ask He knows our needs (Matt 6:8), but He still wants us to ask, for then it will be given to us (Matt 7:7). How abundantly does the heavenly Father give good things to those that ask Him! (Matt 7:11) He invites us to ask Him for whatever we want (John 15:7) and whatever we ask for in His name, *He will do it!* (John 14:14)

Here are some reasons why we *can* ask and *should* ask. Complete these blanks and meditate on these wonderful statements:
John 15:16 Because *Jesus chose us to bear fruit*
John 16:27 Because *we love Jesus*
John 14:13 So that *the Son may bring glory to the Father*
John 16:24 So that *our joy may be complete*

When Jesus prayed, he was heard. When Jesus prayed, God gave Him what He asked. Read Luke 6:12-13 again. Look also at verses 18-20. He prayed so fervently that He carried on right through the night. Next day, He chose the twelve to be the foundations of the Church; the pioneers of a mission that continues to this day. Then He went down to the crowd and extraordinary power was coming from Him to deliver the demonised and to heal the sick. He also preached with great power the tremendous sermon recorded for us. This is what happened to Jesus after a whole night of prayer. And it can still happen to us today.

Waiting Upon The Lord

As we have seen, it is popular to suppose that guidance comes through 'waiting upon the Lord'. This is taken to mean waiting in silence on our knees, seeking to empty our minds of all distracting thoughts so as to allow God to speak to us with His 'still, small voice'. Here is an old poem that expounds this 'holiness' teaching about waiting on God.

> *Wait only upon God; my soul be still*
> *And let thy God unfold His perfect will.*
> *Thou fain would'st follow Him through this year,*
> *Thou fain with listening heart His voice would'st hear.*
> *Thou fain would'st be a passive instrument*
> *Possessed by God, and ever Spirit-sent*
> *Upon His service sweet – be thou still,*
> *For only thus can He in thee fulfil*
> *His heart's desire...*

Freda Hanbury
(Quoted by Andrew Murray in *Waiting on God* c.1895)

The poem was based on Psalm 62:5: "My soul wait in silence for God only" (NASB). Look up this verse in your NIV and copy it out.

Find rest Oh my soul in God alone, my hope comes from him

This reads quite differently. The Hebrew is literally : 'only to-God be-silent my-soul'. Scholars tell us that 'be-silent' means 'to have absolute composure', that is, not being agitated, anxious and fussing about. So the Psalmist is saying, "My soul, be fully composed looking only to God", or "Come on soul, don't fuss about, just look to God." Have a look at the Psalm. You will see that this makes the best sense in the context. It is a call to rest in God's sovereignty rather than a call to try and tune in to God's soft whispers.

Probably the best-known text on this subject is Isaiah 40:31. In the AV it reads, "They that wait upon the Lord shall renew their strength." I was quite surprised when I looked it up in the NIV. Copy out the first part of the verse.

But those who who in the LORD

What have the translators done? Why did they put 'hope' instead of 'wait'?

The Hebrew word 'wait' was sometimes used for robbers lying in wait for a victim. When we have to wait, there is a patient expectancy and an eager anticipation as we look forward in hope to whatever we are waiting for. So the Hebrew word also comes to mean 'hope for'. In current Christian parlance, 'waiting upon' or 'tarrying' indicates the *activity* of quiet prayer, waiting for the Lord to speak or move upon us in some way. But in the scriptures, 'waiting for the Lord' describes an *attitude* of complete trust in God's power to deliver. We demonstrate this confidence in the Lord by patiently waiting for Him to fulfil the promises of His word while we carry on living our lives. This is why the NIV translates it 'hope', which conveys this idea more accurately than 'wait upon', particularly in the light of current terminology.

Here are some other verses all rendered in the AV as 'wait'. Look them up in the NIV: Psalm 25:3,5,21; Psalm 37:9; Psalm 62:1,5.

So we wait for the Lord, *not in order to hear from Him, but because we have been heard by Him.* We wait upon the Lord not *on* our knees but after we have got up *from* our knees. It is patient expectation that rests in God's sovereignty and confidently hopes in Him and, with such an attitude, my! how we gain new strength!

According To His Will
Copy out 1 John 5:14: *This is the confidence we have in approaching God: that if we ask anything according to his will, he hears us.*

How do I know if I am praying according to God's will? Well, is your request scriptural? Is it consistent with what you know of God's desires and purposes revealed in the Bible? When we pray for God's kingdom to come and for the salvation of the lost and the sanctification of the saved, we know we are praying according to His will. An excellent way of making sure that we are praying according to God's will is to actually pray back the scriptures to Him.

How then do we pray for guidance? Not by trying to tune into God's still, small voice, by seeking to 'wait on God' with a blank mind, but by boldly and confidently approaching the throne of grace with a plea for divine wisdom and with specific requests for God to act.

Chapter 7 HEARING GOD'S VOICE

I remember as a child being told the story of the boy Samuel, who heard God calling his name. "Why doesn't God speak to us like that today?" I asked. "We don't need God to speak to us directly", I was told. "We have the Bible today and God speaks to us through that. We can't expect voices from heaven today."

I suppose I accepted that until one day, in my late teens, I was baptised with the Holy Spirit. My heavenly Father, who had always seemed a million miles away in His transcendent holiness, was suddenly there in the room with me in His immanent glory. From that point on I became aware that God communicates with me by His Spirit. I then knew that what I had been told previously was not completely true. Yes, God speaks to us through the Bible, but He also speaks to us in other ways. In fact, one of the most significant things about the Lord is that He is a communicating God (see Deuteronomy 4 verses 7,12,33,36).

Look up the following verses and list the ways in which God speaks: 1 Samuel 3:10-11; Acts 9:4; Daniel 10:12; Matt 2:19; Acts 12:7, 2:17; Matt 1:20; Acts 9:10, 10:17, 16:9, 18:9, 6:10, 13:2, 16:6, 20:23, 21:10-11; 1 Cor 14:3, 25.

Audibly, through other people, angels, visions, dreams, prophesy, by the Holy Spirit,

These are very specific, very clear and very rare! Seldom do we hear audible voices, or have visions of angels. What is more common, however, is the Holy Spirit speaking in prophecy. This is one of a number of similar ways in which the Holy Spirit manifests Himself and speaks to and through us. Other such manifestations include words of wisdom, words of knowledge, tongues and interpretation, discerning of spirits. (1 Cor 12:8-10 AV)

How do these come? They come as 'inward' impressions. They come as thoughts that intrude into our own thoughts, or sudden flashes of insight or revelation. They are indispensable tools in the hands of the experienced counsellor, an essential part of power evangelism, and a regular feature of a church's corporate worship (1 Cor 14:26).

Write out Acts 2:18: *Even on my servants, both men and women, I will pour out my Spirit in those days, and they will prophesy.*

These things are a consequence of being filled with the Spirit. Read 1 Corinthians 12:11 and copy out the last half: *and he gives them to each one just as he determines.*

How do we experience these? Read 1 Corinthians 12:31, 14:1,12,39.

What attitude do we need? *an eager one, zealous*

Why should we want to use such gifts?
to encourage and build up

It is not the scope of this booklet to examine these manifestations of the Spirit in any detail. We shall consider the principles given in the scriptures as to how to handle these, as they relate to God giving us direction or guidance.

Principles of Prophetic Guidance

God may speak when we minister to Him (Acts 13:1-2). If we give ourselves to prayer and ministering to the Lord, He will often give us revelation, and break in with prophetic words. Let us now consider some principles of prophetic guidance.

1. Read 1 Corinthians 14:3. What are the three stated purposes of prophecy?

    1. *strengthening* 2. *encouragement* 3. *comfort*

Notice it does not include admonition, direction, or foretelling the future. While in the Old Testament we have examples of prophecy that pronounces judgement, admonition, direction and foretelling of the future from the mouths of specially chosen and anointed people, in the New Testament the general use of prophecy by ordinary members of the body is limited to these three stated uses. At times a recognised anointed prophet may bring a prophecy that admonishes, gives direction or foretells the future, but they are not part of the normal manifestation of prophecy in which we can all participate to build up the Body of Christ. In church meetings, if someone prophesies and starts admonishing the church or giving strong directive words, the leader will need to rescue the situation because such words can cause all sorts of problems, and be very destructive. The threefold test is simple to apply – write out the three purposes again. Does the prophecy either...*strengthen*...or...*encourage*... or...*comfort*...? If not, correct it!

2. In the Acts passages where prophetic direction was given, it was neither expected nor particularly sought for (see Acts 21:11!). Read Acts 13:1-2. What were these prophets and teachers doing when the prophecy came?
...*worshipping and fasting*...
God will sometimes give His prophets prophecies that are directive or foretelling. How are we to handle them? Copy out 1 Thessalonians 5:19-21: *Do not put out the spirits fire; do not treat prophecies with contempt, test everything. Hold on to the good.*

Here is a very important principle. It is repeated again in 1 Corinthians 14:29. What are other 'prophets' to do?
...*should weigh carefully what is said*...
Copy out 1 John 4:1: *Dear friends do not believe every spirit, but test the spirits to see whether they are from God, because many*

false prophets have gone out into the world

Since we prophesy in part, such prophecies are not authoritative, to be accepted absolutely without question. Both the prophecy itself (the content) and the person who prophesied (the context) need evaluation. As someone has said, "Prophecies are to be weighed, not blindly obeyed."

The context in which I have encountered most directive prophecy and visions has been in leaders' prayer meetings with pastors of churches that work together. In the context of mature, experienced leaders who are based in the reality of day-to-day church leadership and are theologically well grounded, God will give such direction, as in Acts 13. The content is weighed and discussed, prayed through, and slept on before any decisions are made. Generally we must realise the rarity of predictive and directive prophecy. We do not look for it, but when it does come we weigh it carefully and treat it seriously.

3. Another type of prophecy that I have frequently experienced in my calling as a pastor and teacher is 'personal prophecy'. God often gives prophecy at baptisms, when receiving new members, and when ministering to individuals. It is exciting when someone responds by saying that was just what they needed to hear. Such prophecy will accurately relate to their situation and give strength and encouragement to them. Similarly, God will often give words of knowledge and wisdom during times of counselling or prayer for individuals.

How are we to handle personal prophecy? The same threefold test applies: does it strengthen, encourage or comfort? The counsellor should always ask, "Does this mean anything to you? Am I getting it right?" Sometimes they say no! Paul says we prophesy 'in part' and that means we will occasionally get it wrong. We can learn through this and so we must never insist on what we think we have heard! The nature of personal prophecy is encouragement, not to make pronouncements or give new direction. Sometimes you may receive impressions concerning a person's future and direction. Like Mary, treasure these things in your heart and when they later come and share their plans for future direction, you can confirm it for them. I recently shared a change of direction with two close friends, each of whom said, "We've known for a couple of years that you would be making such a move, but it wasn't our place to tell you." That was so right. I am glad they did not pre-empt God's dealings with me by telling me what they had received until the right time, when it became a prophetic confirmation of certain decisions I had had to make.

How to Hear

We must therefore always evaluate the impressions we receive. Some Christians set reason against the Spirit, and there has been a tendency amongst some charismatics to become anti-intellectual and gnostic (claiming special knowledge and putting undue emphasis on supernatural manifestations and visions – see Col 2:18). This is very dangerous. We set our minds on the things of the Spirit (Rom 8:5 in the NASB), so our reason is renewed and agrees with the Spirit.

If we believe our impressions are from the Holy Spirit, then we can safely submit them to reason and to the wisdom of counsellors. This is not quenching or grieving the Spirit (see Eph 4:30, 1 Thess 5:19). The Holy Spirit is not like some timid bird that, if you shout "boo", will fly away! Put Him to the test. He instructs us to do that very thing through the apostle John (1 Jn 4:1). He is pleased to see us meaning business and it safeguards us from deceiving ourselves. Read Acts 17:11 and 2 Thessalonians 2:2.

Again and again we are warned, "Don't be deceived", "Don't let anyone deceive you" (Mk 13:5,22; 1 Cor 3:18, 6:9, 15:33; Gal 6:7; Eph 5:6; 2 Thess 2:3; 2 Tim 3:13; Titus 1:10; Jas 1:16; 1 Jn 1:8, 2:26, 3:7; 2 Jn 1:7). Deception is not something that women are especially vulnerable to, as some perversely imply from 1 Tim 2:14. Anyone is open to deception if they are not submissive to spiritual authority, and if they do not test the spirits, judge prophecy or evaluate their own impressions!

Copy out James 3:17:

But the wisdom that comes from heaven is first of all pure; the peace-loving, considerate, submissive, full of mercy and good fruit, impartial and sincere.

Other translations of the word 'submissive' are: easy to be intreated (AV), open to reason (RSV, NEB), reasonable (NASB), willing to yield (RAV), allows discussion and is willing to yield (LB), and even 'friendly'!! (GNB)

A wise person will not go around saying that God told him to do this or that in a manner that implies an authority that is not open to reason. Rather he will say, "I think the Lord told me. What do you think?" Now this is not a plea for caution but for *wisdom*. We are called to be *wise*, not cautious.

Write out 1 Corinthians 14:1: *Follow the way of love and eagerly desire spiritual gifts, especially the gift of prophecy*

Why are we so strongly encouraged to prophesy? Read Acts 2:17-18 and write out again the last half of verse 18: *and they will prophesy*

We are all encouraged to prophesy because the notable characteristic of God's new covenant people, baptised by Jesus in the Holy Spirit, is that they prophesy! We are a prophetic people through whom God speaks. Prophecy convinces the unbeliever that God is really among us (1 Cor 14:25) and encourages us all to do the will of God. Let us earnestly desire to prophesy, with wisdom and not with caution.

Chapter 8 SIGNS AND WONDERS

Fleeces
One of the popular ways of ascertaining the supposed 'will of God' is by looking for various signs or indicators. This is often referred to as 'putting out a fleece'. For example, I am thinking of selling my car. I do not know if it is God's will for me to get a new one, so I say to God, "I'll advertise it in the local free newspaper and if someone phones up to see it before nine o'clock on the night the paper comes out, I'll take it as a sign that you do want me to buy a new car." This practice is based on the story of Gideon, who put out a fleece in order to get a sign from God. You can find the story in Judges 6:11-40. Read it now, and answer the following questions.
Was Gideon seeking guidance from the Lord when he was in the winepress? ......*No*......

Who initiated the interview between Gideon and the angel of the Lord?
......*The Angel (the LORD)*......

What special task did God have for Gideon to do?
......*To save Israel out of Midian's hands*......

What was Gideon's response when the angel told him about it?
......*My clan is the weakest in Manasseh and I am the least in my family*......

When he put the fleece out the first time, was he trying to discover the will of God? ......*No*...... Why *did* he put it out? ......*To test what he had heard*......

God gave three signs in this chapter (v.21,37,40). Were they supernatural miracles or were they circumstantial happenings?

supernatural

Whose idea was the first sign? _God's_

As you can see, this story has nothing whatsoever to do with our trying to discover what God wants us to do. Gideon knew perfectly well what God had told him to do. He did not need signs to determine what to do; he needed them to buck up his courage because he was too frightened actually to do it! When Gideon put out his fleece, he was not 'putting out a fleece' in the modern popular sense at all. In fact, such a practice of seeking circumstantial indicators is not taught in the scriptures. The only passage in the whole Bible that seemingly gives precedent for such a practice is found in Genesis 24:12-16. Please read the story.

This story describes a most unusual quest: a wife had to be found for this very special son, through whom all the families of the earth would be blessed. This event is not recorded as a pattern for normal living. In verse 7 Abraham told the servant that an angel would go before him to help in his special quest. When he arrived, he prayed because he had no idea how to proceed, and to his amazement God answered immediately. What does this teach us? It shows how much God delights to answer prayer rather than how we should normally proceed in the decision-making process. Even after this remarkable answer to prayer, he did not take the sign as proof. He watched (v.21) and checked her credentials (v.23) before praising God (v.26). Even then the matter was not settled. Were her parents agreeable with the request? (v.49) If not, he would go and look for another girl. Was she willing to go with him? (v.58) Only then did he consider that God had directed him successfully.

Consider it from Rebekah's viewpoint. This was one of those rare sovereign interventions of God. One day she was going about her chores; the next she knew she was caught up in the unexpected purposes of God.

All scripture is written for our instruction, but how are we to apply its lessons to our lives? To make one unique occurrence the basis for a general practice is faulty interpretation. The principles of how to live the Christian life, such as 'how God guides us', are explicitly taught in the scriptures and borne out by various examples, as we have already seen. The idea that God guides through circumstantial signs is neither explicitly taught nor demonstrated by numerous examples. There is, however, one Old Testament practice related to guidance that we need to look at together. It *is* explicitly taught and we have frequent examples, yet it is not practised by those in the new covenant.

Inquiring of the Lord
In the Old Testament we often read of men like David inquiring of the Lord. It was a way of making decisions by asking direct questions of God which always seemed to result in very clear answers and instructions. Some take this to be normative for us today, even though it is absent in the New Testament.

Read 1 Samuel 28:6. In what three ways did King Saul expect God to answer him?
1. *dreams* 2. *Urim* 3. *prophets*
The first and last of these we have already considered in the last chapter. But what is the second? Read Exodus 28:6,15,30. Here we see that the High Priest had a specially designed ephod, attached to which was the breastpiece.
What was the purpose of the breastpiece?
for making decisions; (v.15)
Inside the breastpiece were two objects. What were they called?
Urim and Thummim (v.30)
What was the purpose of the objects contained in the breastpiece?
So that they may be over Aarons heart (v. 30)
Nowhere in the Bible are these objects described for us nor how they were used. In this way, the Lord has made it impossible for anyone in succeeding generations to replicate them for use in decision-making. Turn to 1 Samuel 23:9-12. Here we see that David used this device in making an inquiry of the Lord. It is thought that the objects, whose names mean 'curses' and 'perfections', were used in a similar way to dice. A question was asked, then they were thrown and, depending on how they fell, God's answer was interpreted as either 'yes' or 'no'. So when David asked, "Will you give this people into our hand?", if the Thummim dominated, the answer was understood to be, "I will give this people into your hand"; if

the Urim dominated, it would be read as, "I will not give this people into your hand." (see 2 Sam 2:1)

This form of decision-making is referred to by Solomon in Proverbs 16:33 and is an aspect of the ancient practice of casting of lots. We have examples of it in Judges 20:9, Jonah 1:7 as well as Acts 1:26. We also find that the casting of lots was used to apportion land and to select impartially between different people (e.g. Prov 18:18, Josh 18:8-10, 1 Chron 24:5, Neh 11:1, Luke 1:9). Whenever lots were used to inquire of God, the outcome was recognised as the Lord's decision on the matter. However, Urim and Thummim were not used for ordinary decisions but were kept by the High Priest for occasional use in deciding very serious matters, particularly, it seems, in deciding questions of warfare.

Read 2 Samuel 5:17-25. The commentators suggest that David's regular method of inquiring of God before battles was through the High Priest's ephod, and that the word 'inquire' is a technical term for 'consulting an oracle', which was the Urim and Thummim. What do you notice about the answers God gave in two almost identical situations?

One was just to go the other was more specific.

With which of the following statements would you agree?
1. Because a certain strategy worked once, it does not mean it will automatically work a second time, even if the circumstances are identical.
   TRUE / FALSE
2. David did not act presumptuously but even in a familiar situation he inquired of God.   TRUE / FALSE
3. On the first inquiry (v.19), the wording of the question and answer suggests the use of Urim and Thummim to determine the Lord's instructions.   TRUE / FALSE
4. On the second inquiry, however, it is clear that God spoke to David in some audible way, beyond the capabilities of the ephod. TRUE / FALSE
5. Throwing dice or tossing a coin is a very good way of determining what to do.   TRUE / FALSE
6. We do not need to pray about situations we have handled before.
   TRUE / FALSE

I trust your answers were as follows: True 1,2,3,4. False 5,6.
We see important lessons to be learned from this passage. But what lessons can we learn from Urim and Thummim? How are we to reinterpret their

use in new covenant situations?

Coming of Age

Under the old covenant, God gave the Law and also many very detailed instructions about how the people should build their 'church building', what priests should wear, etc. In the new covenant we are given liberty to decide for ourselves about such things as meeting places and clothing, and how we organise our churches and run our meetings. There are no instructions in the New Testament remotely like those given in the Old.

Paul tells us the purpose of the Law. Write the first half of Gal 3:24:

So the law was put in charge to lead us to Christ

'Was put in charge' translates the Greek word 'pedagogue', which was a personal slave who looked after a young boy. He told him what to do and generally disciplined, guided and looked after the boy until he grew up. He was more of a baby-sitter than a tutor. The old covenant treated people very much as little children. They always had to 'do as they were told'. In Christ, we have come of age. We have left behind the childish need of constantly being told what to do and we have entered a mature Father-son relationship, one of wisdom and advice rather than 'do this, do that' (1 Cor 13:11). When we cry "Abba, Father", we express intimacy rather than immaturity. We have been given a Father-son relationship, not a Daddy-baby relationship.

Urim and Thummim, signs and omens, lots and oracles, dreams, visions and prophets were the stuff of Old Testament baby-sitting. God now calls us to walk with Him in a mature relationship.

We do not need circumstantial signs, fleeces, or any kind of 'yes' and 'no' indications as a means of making decisions. While Proverbs 16:33 is true in terms of God's sovereignty, it does not justify a continuation of the use of lots or signs in decision-making. Christians ought not to toss coins in order to determine 'God's will', but there are some who do!

We should not act presumptuously. In every new situation we need to look to the Lord for fresh wisdom, particularly if we feel 'we've been this way before'. We dare not just act out of habit or tradition. It may have worked last time, but is it the right thing to do now?

When we inquire of God today, we should ask for and expect God to give us wisdom rather than 'yes' or 'no' answers. However, there will be times when the Lord will speak clearly through the scriptures, visions, dreams, voices, angels or prophecy. We must weigh such impressions and submit them to others, but we should not be suspicious or over-cautious.

A Testimony

After studying at university, I worked as a labourer in a factory for two years to gain experience of real life. I was then on the dole for several months, trying unsuccessfully to get into what I thought was a suitable career. One autumn Tuesday, whilst praying with an old school friend, I heard two words: "Try teaching". I turned to my friend. "What did you say?" I asked. "Nothing", he replied. I knew I had heard two clear audible words. They were not in my head. We discussed the voice and what it had said, and so the very next day I went to the local education office. "I would like some information about becoming a school teacher", I said. I only wanted information because I was not sure if I really fancied standing in front of classes of kids! But by Friday I found myself in a school as a maths teacher! The next week was half-term, so I had a week to get used to the idea!

Under ILEA rules, new staff could only be taken on in the first half of a term, and at Christmas new regulations were to come into force. No more teachers would be accepted on the basis of a degree without a professional teaching qualification. That week had been the very last possible opportunity for me to become a teacher without doing an extra year's course. Why did I have to suffer the dole queue for those months? Why did God leave it to the very last moment? Supposing I had not acted on the voice straightaway? Phew!

I know God speaks. I have heard His audible voice. I know God is sovereign. That week I was suddenly propelled into a whole new career that I had not remotely considered. I know I am in God's hands, and through that experience He taught me patience and trust. I gained valuable experience in the factory, on the dole, and in the classroom, all of which has helped me in my ministry as a pastor. Now there have been many other major life-changing decisions that I have made without a word from God, but when God chooses to break in like this, He certainly knows how to do it. It may be very rare but it is certainly very precious.

Chapter 9 TAKING COUNSEL

Turn to Proverbs 15:22 and copy it out:

Plans fail for lack of counsel, but with many advisers they succeed

Similar proverbs are found in 11:14 and 24:6. What two-word phrase is common to all these verses?

many advisers.

Write out Proverbs 20:18:

Make plans by seeking advice; if you wage war, obtain guidance

Those who follow the way of wisdom will only make important decisions after they have talked it through and taken advice from "an abundance of counsellors" (NASB). In the next chapter we shall look at some practical considerations as to how to give and receive such counsel related to decision-making. However, let us firstly look again at Proverbs 11:14. In the original language the sequence of words in this verse reads (without) (wise counsel, guidance, direction) (fall) (the people) (but salvation, deliverance, safety) (in a great, mighty, many) (counsellor). You can see how the NIV translators have arrived at their version but it could equally well be rendered, "Without wise counsel the people fall, but there is salvation in a mighty counsellor."

The Wonderful Counsellor

What mightier counsellor could we have than the Lord Himself? Isaiah calls Jesus the Wonderful Counsellor (Isaiah 9:6). In Him we indeed have salvation, deliverance and safety. In ascending to heaven He gave us His

Holy Spirit to continue this ministry.
Copy out John 14:16:

And I will ask the Father, and he will give you another Counsellor to be with you for ever

When Jesus spoke of 'another' counsellor, the word used in our Greek N.T. indicates another one of the same kind rather than another different one. The Holy Spirit is not different to Jesus, He is a Counsellor exactly like Jesus Himself. He is the very Spirit of Jesus. The title 'Counsellor' or 'Helper' (NASB) indicates one who comes alongside us to help and comfort, to fortify and to encourage us.

So as well as providing many counsellors, He has given us the mightiest of all counsellors, who is the very Spirit of His Son. So how does the Counsellor guide us and keep us safe?

Led by the Spirit
Copy out Romans 8:14:

because those who are led by the Spirit of God are sons of God.

and Galatians 5:18:

But if you are led by the Spirit, you are not under law

Read the context of each of these verses. Is Paul speaking of decision-making or moral behaviour?

moral behaviour

Clearly the Holy Spirit primarily leads us into doing the will of God, living holy lives and fulfilling the law from our hearts. What does John tell us He leads us or guides us into in John 16:13?

into all truth.

Again we see that the guidance that the Counsellor gives us is in areas of character, responses and behaviour. He convinces us of sin, righteousness and judgment (John 16:8), and enables us to do the will of God. This is the kind of counsel He gives us. When we read of 'those who are led by the Spirit' we need to understand it in terms of leading us in the paths of righteousness rather than directing us as to what decisions to make in non-moral areas, as we have already seen in Chapter 1.

The Spirit leads into the truth, opening our minds to understand the Bible and reminding us of relevant scriptures which we saw in Chapter 2. However, we certainly need the help of the Holy Spirit when we have decisions to make. How does the Counsellor counsel us in such situations?

Write out the common phrase in the following verses: Deut 34:9, Is 11:2, Eph 1:17:

The Spirit of Wisdom

Why do you suppose Stephen was full of wisdom? (Acts 6:3):

(answer is a supposition)

When we are full of the Holy Spirit, we are filled with the *Spirit of Wisdom*, for that is where we get our wisdom from. When we pray and ask God for wisdom, He actually gives us His own Spirit of wisdom and insight and understanding, as we saw in Chapters 5 and 6. By that same Spirit we receive words of wisdom or prophetic insight from time to time, or He may break in upon us with a dream or a vision which we will need to test and submit to others to confirm that it is truly of God. We have already considered this in Chapters 7 and 8, and have seen how this is initiated out of God's sovereignty, but how it only comes to those who eagerly desire such manifestations, who are open to being used of God and seeking to go on being filled with the Holy Spirit. Have you been filled with the Spirit? If so, do you make sure you keep on being filled with the Spirit? If not, seek prayer and counsel, for God intends each of us to live full of His Spirit.

The Witness of the Spirit

Perhaps you are saying, "You haven't mentioned the 'witness of the Spirit' which is surely the main way in which the Spirit guides us in non-moral decisions." You might believe so when you read the popular books on guidance, but not when you read the Bible! The phrase is based on Romans 8:16, which in the AV/NASB uses the word 'witness'. This means the same as the word 'testifies' in the NIV. Copy out this verse from the NIV:

The Spirit himself testifies with our spirit that we are the children of God.

Does this have anything to do with guidance? YES / NO.
Another passage that speaks of the witness of the Spirit in the AV or NASB is 1 John 5:6-11. Read this through in the NIV. What does the Holy Spirit testify to? *God has given us eternal life, and this life is in his Son.*

The only other passage that could possibly give rise to the expression 'witness of the Spirit' is Hebrews 10:15 (AV or NASB), and again you can see that the context has to do with salvation, not guidance. The witness of the Holy Spirit with our spirit has nothing to do with decision-making but has to do with assurance of salvation. It is that wonderful conviction of God's love poured into our hearts so that we really know we are children of God. This experience of the witness of the Spirit comes to us when we are baptised or filled with Him. It is 'joy unspeakable and full of glory'. How then does the phrase 'witness of the Spirit' come to be used in the context of guidance if it is not used like that in the scriptures? It has come about through the experiences of Christians. However, if you read the examples given in many of the books, they fall mainly into two categories:
1. Divine promptings, such as 'divine appointments', often with remarkable results. These would be Spirit-initiated directives such as we have already considered in the chapter on signs and wonders (Chapter 8).
2. Strong warnings from the Spirit not to take certain actions.

Turn to Acts 20:23. Write out this verse from your NIV:
I only know that in every city the H/S warns me that prison and hardships are ...

This warning of the Spirit is not an uncommon experience amongst Christians. A Christian businessman was about to sign a multi-million pound contract, having researched the market thoroughly. It was an excellent deal and was expected to make a huge profit. But he could not sleep. Every time he turned the deal over in his mind it all seemed so good, yet he had an inner irrational sense of alarm that he could not escape. Next day he turned down the contract, saying he had prayed about it and did not feel happy. They all ridiculed him, but within one year the bottom had unforeseeably fallen out of the market. Had he signed he would have lost everything and ended up in bankruptcy. This is a classic example of the warning bells the Spirit sometimes sets off within us when we are about to make a decision. It may seem a very wise decision, given all the information, but God alone knows the future and those events, consequences and dangers that we cannot possibly foresee.

We do not know quite how the Holy Spirit warned Paul in Acts 16:6-7. It may well have been through some sort of strong irrational inner disturbance. Read these verses and write down what it says the Holy Spirit did in these two instances.

Stopped them from preaching in Asia & didn't allow them to enter Bithinium

However, in the example we already read in Acts 20:22-23 the warnings came prophetically (see also Acts 21:10-15). The Lord forewarned Paul of what to expect in Jerusalem. But Paul had a sense of compulsion that despite God's warnings would not permit him to avoid the dangers. The warnings did not change his decision to go to Jerusalem. Rather he would face the dangers forewarned and forearmed.

The Peace of God

This occasional experience of warning has unfortunately been turned into a general doctrine. If we have to make a decision and we do not feel disturbed, we then have a 'sense of peace'. This sense of peace, or lack of a troubled spirit, is identified wrongly as 'the witness of the Spirit'. People often say that the witness of the Spirit is that sense of inner peace, the peace of God, that rules in our hearts to confirm that our decisions are according to God's will. This 'inner peace' is sought as a subjective arbiter in our decision-making. It is taken as a green light, and 'lack of peace' as a red light in *all* decisions. While God occasionally intervenes with warnings of various kinds, we cannot make it into a general principle. But many teach the need for 'the peace of God' as an essential signpost in matters of guidance on the basis of texts such as Colossians 3:15. This is how the Amplified Bible translates it: "And let the peace (soul harmony which comes) from the Christ rule (act as umpire continually) in your hearts – deciding and settling with finality all questions that arise in your minds – (in that peaceful state) to which (as members of Christ's) one body you were also called (to live)...." This may be taken to imply a sense of inner harmony that helps us to decide in various non-moral questions. Hence this passage is often taken to teach the need to have an inner arbiter, i.e. a sense of inner peace, that indicates "yes, do that", or a lack of peace that indicates "no, don't do it." In other words a sort of inner spiritual Urim and Thummim. Look up Colossians 3:12-17. In the context, what does peace mean? Is it

A. inner harmony within the person, or
B. harmony between persons?   A/B

As you can see, it actually has nothing to do with guidance or decision-making at all! It is totally concerned with inter-personal relationships. It is a peace-loving attitude that Christ gives us in our hearts to enable us to live peaceably with one another. Paul is saying, let this rule you rather than letting conflict and grievances rule you.

Another passage about peace is Philippians 4:6-7. This *is* speaking about an inner sense of harmony but in this case 'peace' means a freedom from anxiety. It transcends understanding and it guards our hearts and minds. Consider a situation where someone is anxious about some matter. What does this passage tell them to do?

Do not .... *be anxious* ....

but...present .... *your requests to God* ....

In what three ways are they to do this?

1. *prayer*   2. *petitions*   3. *thanksgiving*

This is again not primarily in the context of guidance or decision-making. All sorts of situations may cause anxiety, and peace is freedom from anxiety. It is a supra-rational sense of well-being that comes from confidence in God. It is the consequence of resting in God's sovereignty and of trusting and hoping in God. It is not an inner YES-NO indicator for decision-making. Copy out Isaiah 26:3:

You will keep in perfect peace him whose mind is steadfast, because he trusts in you.

Now of course decision-making may be the cause of anxiety. We often do worry about decisions that have to be made. What does Paul tell us to do in such situations? We make our requests to God: "Lord, help me to make this decision; give me your wisdom", and then talk it out in prayer. Afterwards we get up from our knees peaceful and no longer full of anxiety, and that peace of God continues to guard our hearts as we make our plans and as they are implemented.

Chapter 10 MANY COUNSELLORS

The passages in Proverbs that we looked at in Chapter 9 speak about taking advice from human counsellors. These may not be so wonderful as the Lord Himself but the Holy Spirit uses other people, even non-Christians, to give us the counsel that we need. We have seen that God is a speaking God; all through history He has communicated with His people. But a significant aspect of this communication is the way in which the Lord so often used spokesmen.

Copy out Hebrews 3:7:

So as the H/S says: "If you hear his voice..."

In this quotation from Psalm 95 the Holy Spirit speaks through the unknown Psalmist concerning the Israelites whom Moses brought out of Egypt. They 'heard the voice of God' but they rebelled and were judged by the Lord. But in what sense did they hear God's voice?

What they actually heard were the words of God's spokesmen, such as Moses, Samuel or some other prophet. On one occasion at Sinai where God's voice is actually heard by the people (see Exodus 19 and 20 and Deuteronomy 5), it is clear that what the people heard was only a voice-like sound, something like thunder (cf. Job 37:2-4). It was Moses who actually stood between God and the people and relayed the words of the ten commandments to them.

Write out Hebrews 1:1:

In the past God spoke to our forefathers through the prophets at many times & in various ways.

In Matthew 23:34 Jesus speaks of three groups of 'spokesmen'. What are they?
1. *prophets* 2. *wise men* 3. *teachers*

Under the new covenant we all know the Lord for ourselves (Jeremiah 31:34) and can each recognise the voice of the Shepherd (John 10:27). However, God still speaks to us from time to time through other people, particularly through prophets, wise men and teachers.

Write out Hebrews 13:17: *Obey your leaders and submit to their authority. They keep watch over you as men who must give an account. Obey them so that their work will be a joy, not a burden, for that would be of no advantage to you.*

The word translated 'obey' in this verse is not the usual one that means 'do as you're told'. Rather it means 'listen to them, be persuaded by them and follow their leadership out of conviction'. It underlines the importance of having an open, teachable heart, ready to be entreated and willing to be persuaded. What a great joy it is for church leaders to know they have the hearts of their people in this way! This special voluntary relationship between pastors and people is a particularly tender example of being under authority. A Christian with this sort of heart-attitude, when faced with an important decision, will firstly want to listen to what counsel his leaders, as 'prophets, wise men and teachers', have to give.

On a wider front God puts us all in situations where 'chains of command' operate. In the home there is the leadership of husbands and fathers. In our jobs we have bosses and managers; in school, teachers and in society, policemen and government officials. Look up and read the following verses: 1 Peter 2:13,18, 3:1, 5:5. Scripture is very clear as to what our response should be to all God-given leadership. What is that?

to be submissive.

(See also Eph 5:22,24; 6:1-3, 5-6; Col 3:18,20,22; Tit 2:9,3:1) Read Romans 13:1-2. From where do those in authority get that authority?

from God.

Therefore we must *recognise God's authority* in them, whether they are Christians or not. Thus we can be confident that God works sovereignly in those who are over us – our husbands, parents, bosses, teachers, elders, leaders and the government. Even if they are 'harsh', we are ultimately in God's hands and not theirs. We can afford to submit because when we do so God blesses us and works in the situation. It is when we kick against authority that we get ourselves into problems, because that is a violation of God's will. We need to recognise that despite human fallibility and weakness, God speaks to us and blesses us through those He has put over us, and that to heed their counsel is to listen to God.

Some Practical Guidelines
1. When others make decisions that affect you or that you have to implement, do God's will by co-operating joyfully. A critical spirit, reluctance and complaining in such situations are sinful. Trust in God's power to overrule in any decision you may deem unwise and pray for God to work in it (see Ruth 3:5).
2. If you are instructed to do something that is wrong and therefore not God's will, how should you handle it? For example, a father tells a child to answer the phone and say, "Dad's not at home." Or a boss tells his secretary to tell a client that the matter is being dealt with when you know full well it is still sitting on the desk unattended to! Or your manager tells you not to include certain items liable for VAT on the VAT invoice. Ask God for wisdom, "Help, Lord!" and seek some creative alternative that maintains your integrity, such as, "I'm sorry, Dad's not available to talk to you at the moment", or, "I'm sorry that there has been a hold-up, but I will chase it up and make sure you get it as soon as possible." A Biblical example of a creative alternative is found in Daniel 1:8-16.
3. Sometimes, however, you may be told to do something illegal or immoral and can find no alternative except to say, "Sorry, I'm a Christian. I cannot do that." You may have to suffer for that by being ostracised, penalised, or even losing your job. Nevertheless, you have kept your integrity and pleased the Lord by doing His will. Since He did not provide a way of escape, you can trust that, in His sovereignty, God has some other purpose to fulfil in permitting this to happen to

you (see Daniel 3).
4. When a major decision has to be made, we usually need help in making that decision. Proverbs tells us to consult with "many advisers". This means everyone who is relevant to the decision and can throw necessary light upon the situation. Who are our wise men and teachers?
   a) Those with insight, who know the scriptures in depth and can shed light upon the will of God for us.
   b) Those with responsibility and authority over us, including non-Christians, such as bosses or parents, particularly when the decision relates to them in some way (e.g. job moves, marriage, etc.)
   c) Those with personal experience, who have faced similar decisions themselves. The lessons they learned and the experience they gained may be helpful in our own situations.
   d) Those with specialist knowledge, again including non-Christians. We need to consult them in decisions relating to such things as finance, property, buying appliances or items like cars. Remember: "Wisdom counts the cost" (see Luke 14:28-32).
   e) Those who know us intimately and can help us to see our blind spots.
5. It is important to make *your own* decisions. Weigh up what others say – but do not ask them to make the decision for you. Ask them, "What do you think?" rather than, "What would you do?" Go away and talk over with the Lord all the counsel you have heard. Make a confident decision and pray for its successful outcome.

A Word to Leaders

1. "Obey your leaders and submit to their authority." Thus we read in Hebrews 13:17. But this is clearly not a licence for authoritarianism or paternalism. The scope of a leader's authority is in bringing Biblical teaching and injunction to those under his charge. He counsels, exhorts, admonishes and instructs them to do the will of God as written in the Word of God, not by laying down the law, but by grace bringing about the obedience of faith. As leaders, our main purpose is to help those we are responsible for to build godly character,

responses and behaviour into their lives, so that they may more fully do the will of God.

2. In the area of non-moral decisions, we should take great care not to make other people's decisions for them or to tell them what to do. We must studiously avoid saying, "I would do this if I were you." We must realise that as leaders our words carry power. Even our casual remarks can be taken very seriously by others. We must never take people aside and make casual directive comments: "I believe this of you." Like prophecy, directive counsel if it is wrong can tie a person up for years.

   The best way to help someone is to ask pertinent questions which enable them to unwrap the issues and highlight the pros and cons. Throughout the interview, ask God for His wisdom in helping the person, keeping an ear open for any insight the Spirit may give you. Instruct them in the principles of decision-making, especially if they are concerned about missing God's will or trying to 'hear from God'. Lead them to the place of confident, prayerful decision-making. When they come back and tell us what they have decided, then we can confirm it by saying, "Great, that's exactly what I would have done." (Hopefully!)

3. When making decisions that affect others (like choosing people to undertake various tasks), always make such decisions corporately. Plurality safeguards us from locking people up in unsuitable tasks. Do not pronounce: "We believe the Lord would have you take responsibility for this area of church life." Enter into dialogue – "What do you think about this..?" Affirm and encourage – "I think you could do the job well" – and allow *them* to make the decision. Once they have 'bought it', then they will 'own it'. However, always leave them a way out, perhaps by allowing a trial period (see 1 Tim 3:10).

   In wider church decisions, dialogue is essential. Talk, listen, watch, reflect and share as widely as possible. Publicly teach, explain and prepare so that when the final decision comes, everyone has already anticipated it and therefore already owns it. They feel as if they had made the decision themselves and your pronouncement confirms that they were right.

Contra-indications

Have you ever seen this written on a medicine bottle? It means that the medicine is unsuitable for those suffering from the stated complaints. Here are complaints that make the taking of 'much counsel' quite unsuitable.

a) Hypersensitivity. A violent reaction to the counsel given by their leaders that causes them to look around for more palatable counsel.

b) Manipulation. This occurs when a decision has already been made with the knowledge that it is not the best or wisest one. The case is repeatedly presented to numerous people (in a distorted way) in order to obtain sufficient agreement or confirmation of the decision so as to salve a bad conscience.

c) Rapacity. Those with this condition thrive on attention. By going from person to person they satisfy something of their sinful self-indulgence. The longer they can put off making their decision, the longer they can enjoy talking about it.

d) Dipsychosis. An inability to make one's own decisions. Such double-minded people are always looking for someone else to make their decisions for them. Even then they do not really trust the decision, so they constantly look around for confirmation from everyone else.

The general treatment for these complaints is a recognition that these are sin, a sincere repentance, and a resolve henceforth to walk by the Spirit in the way of wisdom.

Chapter 11 VOCATION AND MARRIAGE

In Chapters 11 to 13 we shall look at five major areas in which we frequently struggle in making decisions. These are:
- Vocation
- Marriage
- Church
- Ministry
- Home.

We shall very briefly look at some of the principles relating to these areas, but it is not my intention to give you all the counsel you need in this little booklet. For a start, that is impossible because, while we can look at some general principles, the specific ingredients in each situation are diverse and unique. It is therefore *absolutely essential* that in these areas *you begin to take counsel from your church leaders at the very earliest stage*. It is foolishness to wait until you have more or less made up your mind and then make an appointment to see your pastor or elder. As soon as you begin to think about moving or changing jobs or seriously developing a relationship, *go and talk to your pastor*. He will not tell you what to do, but he will help you to see the issues clearly and set you on a pathway that will lead to a wise and godly decision.

These five areas are the most life-changing decisions we have to make, apart from the greatest of all, which was to follow Christ. One small decision now can affect the course of our lives for years to come. Being aware of the seriousness of such decisions can create enormous uncertainty and stress, and there is often a nagging fear, "Have I done God's will? Was this really what God wanted me to do?" I hope we have blown away the insubstantial fabric of such fears and that we can move into a position of wise, confident, expectant decision-making in these big ones!

VOCATION

In our society today we have an extraordinary breadth of choice when thinking about education and employment, from deciding GCSE options through to decisions about job moves. Hundreds of years ago the sort of work you did depended largely on your class and background; there was comparatively little choice and it seemed almost pre-ordained that you went 'into service' or 'worked the land' or 'took up the family business'. This predetermined flow of society that preserved the structure from generation to generation was a feature of life in Bible days. Copy out the first question contained in these two verses:

Matthew 13:55 *Isn't this the carpenter's son?*

Mark 6:3 *Isn't this the carpenter.*

Jesus had no difficulty choosing a career – He was apprenticed by His father and simply took over the business when he died, along with His brothers, who no doubt carried on when He took off to become a travelling preacher. The fishermen, James and John, Andrew and Peter, were sons of fishermen – they were brought up to the task. So in Biblical days there was comparatively little choice of career, apart from a few examples, such as the enterprising Matthew, who saw his chance of self-betterment by getting in with the Roman overlords and collecting taxes for them.

Does this mean that the scriptures have nothing to say to the problems we face in a modern technological and egalitarian society? Not at all. Look up the following verses and write down, in your own words, the *principles* you consider relevant to our present situation.

2 Thess 3:6-12 *It doesn't matter what type of work you do as long as you do actually work for a living. Don't be idle about work.*

1 Timothy 5:8 *Man should provide for his family, he must work*

Eph 4:28 *must do something useful within our hands, must work, get a job*

2 Corinthians 6:14 ....

Eph 6:7-8 *serve as if serving the Lord, work like you were doing it for the Lord Jesus Christ*

Col 3:23 *work hard as you would for the Lord*

In this last verse we have a similar phrase to the one we looked at in Ecclesiastes 9:10 – "Whatever you do" or "Whatever your hand finds to do". The general thrust of all these passages is – *it does not really matter what you do as long as you are engaged in some gainful employment and thus fulfilling your responsibilities, and whatever you do, make sure you are pleasing God.* Some jobs are simply not suitable for Christians. We could not conceive of a Christian burglar or prostitute or drug dealer or protection racketeer. However, there are jobs with less obvious dangers than these and we need to check them out pretty thoroughly. For example, will there be pressure to act unrighteously in this job? Will I have to sell my soul to the company in a way that is unreasonable for me as a Christian? Will it demand a change in my priorities – God first, family second, church third, job fourth? Will going into partnership with unbelievers be dangerous and compromise my position as a believer?

Round pegs in round holes
Copy out 1 Peter 4:10:

Each one should use whatever gift he has to serve others faithfully, administering God's grace in its various forms.

While this specifically refers to spiritual gifts within the Church the principle is helpful on a wider front. How can I best use the gifts and abilities that God has given me?

Further education develops gifts we already have and equips us better. It cannot make up for deficiencies in ability. Therefore students should go for what they are good at, what they like and enjoy, rather than pursue some ideal or follow some unrealistic ambition (e.g. parental ambitions for a child to become a doctor or an accountant or a minister). In making such decisions we need the counsel of others who can view us more objectively than we can ourselves.

When having to make decisions about jobs:
1. *use God's wisdom*
2. *take good counsel*
3. *pray yourself into a suitable job*

so that you will be able to provide for yourself (and family and others), and fully use your capabilities to serve the Lord. How satisfying it is to be in a job which is God's answer to your prayers and His response to the desires of your heart.

MARRIAGE

Considering marriage, we again see how very different modern society is from that of Biblical times. In those days the majority of marriages were arranged for sons and daughters by concerned parents who ensured that their offspring married suitable partners, of appropriate background, nationality and status. We do have a few Biblical examples of 'falling in love', e.g. Jacob and Rachel in Genesis 29:18-19. Please read this story.

Now if we read further we gain a fascinating insight into God's view of love and marriage. Read Genesis 29:31-35.

What did God expect of Jacob in his marriage to Leah?

to love Leah; to love her, be attached to her.

Write out Ephesians 5:25:

Husbands love your wives just as Christ loved the church and gave himself up for her.

Read verse 33 also. Clearly love is the duty of the husband, whoever he is married to. In our culture the idea of arranged marriage is quite unacceptable, but as Tevye's wife replies to her husband's question, "Do you love me?" in *Fiddler on the Roof*: "My father and my mother said we'd learn to love each other and after twenty-five years, I suppose I do!" This is a Biblical expectation, especially in Christian marriage, that love is the fruit of marriage, not particularly the grounds of marriage.

So what then are the grounds of marriage? Does God have the ideal wife for each person? It is often said at wedding services that "marriages are made in heaven", and we often thank God that "He has brought these two people together." But in what sense is that true?

Choosing a Partner
We have already seen that the story of Abraham's servant who goes to find a wife for Isaac does *not* teach a general principle that God has a preordained perfectly complimentary partner for each individual and all we have to do is follow the signposts until we find each other. On the contrary, the overwhelming tenor of the scriptures is that *Christians are free to marry anyone they wish* (see 1 Cor 7:39) with one exception. Write out the first sentence of 2 Corinthians 6:14:

Do not be yoked together with unbelievers.

What is the one proviso as far as a marriage partner is concerned?

Must be born again.

In Bible days parents judged the suitability of a partner. Today we have to do that largely for ourselves. It is important to talk to parents, pastors and friends about our thoughts and feelings towards the other person at an early stage. While we cannot 'miss God's perfect will' (because such a blueprint does not exist) and end up with a partner who is God's second best, we can marry someone without sufficient understanding of the problems we will cause one another. If we go into marriage on the basis of romance or sexual attraction without a mutual commitment to do God's will, we can create a problem that will last for the rest of our lives! Sadly, even Christian marriages sometimes end in divorce. It need not be so if we are careful in choosing our partner, and that once we are married we are both determined to do the will of God, which means the husband loving his wife sacrificially and the wife honouring and obeying her husband as the Lord. Any couple who live like this will have a marriage that is a roaring success.

Here, first of all, are some obvious questions to ask:
- Do we click?
- Do we like each other?
- Do we get on well together?
- Do we have a good friendship?
- Can we talk to each other?
- Do we have sufficient things in common?
- Do we have sufficient differences to complement and need one another?
- Are we attracted to each other?

And now here are some very important questions which must not be forgotten:
- Do we have the same values?
- Do we have the same spiritual desires?
- Are we equally committed to the Church?
- Will this person help me to grow spiritually or be a drain on me?
- Will I be able to have spiritual input to them or do they resist it?
- Do either of us intimidate the other or make each other feel inferior?
- Would it be possible for either of us to be abused by the other?
- Do we accept each other as we are, or would either of us find ourselves continually critical of the other and seeking to change the other?
- Would we be able lovingly to give correction to and receive it from one another?
- Could we manage to run a home together?
- Do we have common goals and desires (e.g. having a family, home, ministry to others)?
- Do we have compatible jobs or would our career interests come between us?
- Do we recognise the difficulties we may face if we marry and are we committed to one another sufficiently to work through all of these problems?

To Marry or Not to Marry

This begs the question, should I even marry at all? While marriage was ordained by God from creation, it is wrong to conclude that celibacy is unnatural or that the unmarried are somehow deficient. It is sometimes stated that in Genesis 2:18 God is affirming the incompleteness of man and woman apart from each other, and that marriage is the God-given means of achieving completeness. But what does Genesis 2:18 actually say?

It is not good for man to be alone, I will make a helper suitable for him.

Alone does *not* mean incomplete. Each one of us is a complete human being, yet none of us is sufficient in ourselves. We need others, but that does not mean we *must* marry! We are social beings who need one another and such needs can be met through family and close friends as well as through marriage. Jesus and Paul, who were both unmarried, present celibacy as something good. It is neither better than nor inferior to marriage, but equally valid and profitable. Those who choose it should do so for the sake of the Kingdom, and those who find themselves unmarried should accept it for the sake of the Kingdom. Read 1 Corinthians 7:28,32-35. Notice Paul's expediency. Is it wise to marry? Well, we will have to weigh it up. If we choose not to marry, what a great advantage we have over married people! Single people do have to cope with the difficulties of loneliness and sexual desires at times, but over and against that what does Paul say in v.28?

we will be spared many troubles in this life

It is important that the local church ethos does not disadvantage either the married or the single. A certain church led by an unmarried pastor took 1 Corinthians 7:32-33 so literally that they only had single people in leadership and married people were considered 'too concerned about the affairs of this world' to be given church responsibilities! Conversely, there are churches where the ethos is so heavily flavoured by married elders, deacons and housegroup leaders (see 1 Tim 3:2,4,5,12) that the unmarried are considered lacking in 'a basic maturity and understanding that can only come through the responsibilities of marriage and family life'. In such a church singles feel redundant, unutilised and unfulfilled (particularly single women). They are made to feel that the only way to grow and find fulfilment is to marry and have children! Neither of these scenarios is scriptural nor helpful.

Read l Corinthians 7:1-9 and Matthew 19:10-12. Note especially verse 7 in the first and verse 11 in the second passage. What essential requirement do we need if we choose not to marry?

that particular gift

This is a gift from God, of self-restraint and self-sufficiency, that enables a person to live a fulfilled single life. What does Paul say in l Corinthians 7:9?

If they cannot control themselves, they should marry, for it is better to marry than to burn with passion.

How can we handle that? Firstly, we must 'flee from immorality' and secondly, *pray* for a suitable partner. When God answers this prayer, sometimes after many years, we can then truly say the marriage 'was made in heaven' and take delight in the one who was an answer to prayer.

78

Chapter 12 CHURCH

We have already noted how very different society is today from that of New Testament times. Perhaps the most disturbing difference between the world today and that of the apostles is the extraordinary proliferation of churches that we now have. In New Testament days there would be no question as to what church to go to, because there was only one church in each city or town where the gospel had reached. All the Christians in that locality were part of that one local community.

Today in England the local parish church would not gather all the local believers. It could be anything from high Anglo-Catholic to lively charismatic evangelical via deadly liberal! In addition, there are likely to be various alternative local free churches. These will either have broken away or been established autonomously over the past centuries or recent decades. Some of these would be even worse than a dead Church of England. All of these are called 'churches', but their very existence highlights the fact that there is a very wide diversity of opinion over what constitutes a church.

When is a Church not a Church?
Read Colossians 1 verses 18 and 24. What is the Church?

The body of Christ

Write out 1 Corinthians 12:27:

Now you are the body of Christ and each of you is a part of it.

Clearly then, the Church is *people*. It is not a building, but a group of Christians who have come together.

Write out the first half of 1 Corinthians 11:18:

In the first place, I hear that when you come together as a church.

Notice Paul says 'when you come together *as* a church' not *in* church. Indeed, the very word translated 'church' means an assembly of people; those that have been called out or summoned together.

However, this is not just an *ad hoc* gathering of Christians. Turn back to 1 Corinthians 12:27 which you copied above, but now read verse 28. Copy it up to 'teachers':

And in the church God has appointed first of all apostles, second prophets, third teachers,

The Church is a gathered Christian community under appointed spiritual leadership. Who appoints these ministries?

God

Look in Acts 20 verse 17. Who does he send for?

The elders

What does he say about them in verse 28 (first half)?

that the HS has made them overseers.

What does he tell them to be in verse 28 (second half)?

Shepherds of the church of God.

'Elders' emphasises maturity and wisdom, 'overseers' stresses the responsibility to watch over the flock and 'shepherds' depicts the practical task of feeding and caring for the members of the church. Who made these men overseers of the church?

The Holy Spirit.

How did that happen? It happened through recognition of their gifting and appointment to the task by men such as Paul, Barnabas and Titus (see Acts 14:23 and Titus 1:5), probably by laying on of hands in front of the church (see Acts 6:6 and 1 Tim 4:14, 5:22).

A church then is only a church if it is composed of genuine believers and if it has properly established and appointed spiritual leadership, who faithfully teach the Word of God and lead the church according to God's Word. There are so-called 'churches' led by unconverted ministers, or made up of religious but unconverted people. These are not churches in the New Testament sense at all.

Joining a Church

If you are moving or looking to join a new church, here are some questions to ask:
- Does the church believe in the inspiration of the scriptures and seek to base all its teaching and practice upon the scriptures?
- Does the church expect people to experience conversion and does it only accept as members those who show signs of genuine new birth?
- Are the leaders spiritually minded and godly men, themselves accountable to others, that the church happily follows?
- Is the church subject to the Holy Spirit? Are there spiritual gifts exercised during its meetings? Is there true worship and are people encouraged to go on being filled with the Spirit?
- Does the church preach the Gospel, teach the Word, properly administer baptism and breaking of bread, and exercise church discipline where necessary?
- Does the church have good relations with other churches and does it have an open-hearted attitude of unity with all believers, free from exclusiveness?

Now most people join a new church because they were converted through the church or because they have just moved into the area. We shall look at the second of these in the latter part of the next chapter. I want to look now at the more serious guidance problems: "I'm feeling unhappy in my local church. Is it right to leave this church and go to another one?"

When Is It Right to Leave?
    a) When you cannot accept the theological stance or practical structuring of the church. You do not agree with what is taught or like the way things are run. You can see glaring weaknesses and errors and feel that there ought to be different emphases and that changes need to be made. If you stay you will inevitably cause trouble, undermine the leadership and create division. You will be an unwitting tool in

Satan's hand. You need to leave quietly and amicably, and find a church where they hold the same values, theology and philosophy of ministry as you do. If you cannot find anywhere to your liking, then you seriously need to evaluate your own attitudes and views.

Amos 3:3 states an obvious principle. "How can two walk together unless they agree?" Copy this from the NIV:

Do two walk together unless they have agreed to do so?

Israel were unfaithful covenant-breakers. They adopted values and practices quite different to those prescribed by the Lord, yet still claimed allegiance to Him, and complained at God's judgments against them. As the Lord points out, we cannot walk together in harmony in the same direction unless we hold the same values, keep faith with one another in a covenant commitment and agree to walk together in the same direction in mutual support and co-operation. This sort of commitment is essential to the success of a local church.

b) When you really cannot relate to any of the leaders. Being part of a church means having a relationship with and respect for the leaders, and if you do not like any of them and find them all difficult, you will not be able to submit to them so as to make their responsibility a joy. Find a church with leaders you do click with. If you cannot find anywhere to your liking, you need to take a serious look at your own attitudes and reactions.

c) When something has happened to you that demands a fresh start in a different situation. e.g.
- you have just been baptised in the Spirit and pray in tongues but the church is anti-charismatic.
- you have backslidden and feel very awkward about going back to the church where you were once so actively involved.
- you have fallen into immorality or an unhealthy relationship with another church member; you have both repented but you now need to move away from that person to avoid further temptation.

Do talk to the leaders first about your move.

d) When you feel you have been around long enough and it is time to move on into a fresh situation, where you will face fresh challenges and be able to use all you have learned from your present church. It is preferable to move on into a new location rather than switch to another local church. Look to be directed to a new church planting, or a small work that needs some good servant-hearted established Christians to strengthen it.

When Is It Wrong to Leave?

a) When you feel unhappy or confused because you have been the sounding board for other people's moans, criticisms and gripes. You were quite happy with the leadership and direction of the church until the failings of the leaders and things lacking in the church were pointed out to you. Now you feel thoroughly dissatisfied and feel like getting out. Don't! Go and talk to the leaders and stop listening to the complainers, but rather do the will of God. Such critics ought to go. Unfortunately they often hang on until they have done a lot of damage, and then write a warm letter to the elders: "We feel the Lord is leading us to new pastures and the time has now come for us to resign our membership." Often they sound so pleasant, so caring, so plausible, but their words drip away like vitriol and eat right into the lives of all who get close to them. Proverbs 24:21 warns us not to associate with those who press for change. Copy the verse out from the NIV:

Fear the LORD and the King, my son, and do not join with the rebellious.

Wanting to see change, more of God's presence, greater vision, more liberty and better pastoral care sounds very good but it can easily be a form of rebellion. This inevitably happens when, instead of supporting the leadership in the changes they are seeking to implement, a person either resists change or criticises the lack of more radical measures. Any member who distances himself from the leadership and adopts a 'them' and 'us' mentality will create division in the local church and their leaven may infect the whole lump. Read the story in Numbers 16.

b) When you have been corrected or disciplined and find yourself reacting to difficult counsel given to you; or when you are removed from a job or not given a job (such as housegroup leader) and feel hurt, rejected, upset or angry with the leaders. "No discipline seems pleasant at the time but painful." Turn to this verse, Hebrews 12:11, and write out the benefits we get from discipline, providing, that is, we receive it and respond humbly and correctly to it:

It produces a harvest of righteousness and peace.

c) When you feel neglected or uncared for; or when the housegroup leader is OK but the pastor never talks to you; or when you have a problem you need to talk about but you cannot bring yourself to go and see one of the leaders, and no one comes to you and asks how you are. All of these typical feelings and reactions can come to us at times. They are always caused by our unreasonable expectations of others. We must learn to overcome the temptations to self-pity, embarrassment or fear, and if we have needs, we must actually ask for help. If we just drift off and leave the church we take the same harmful behaviour patterns with us to a new church. If we do not get these feelings out into the open quickly, they fester and turn into a root of bitterness that becomes impossible to heal and sadly leads to unnecessary separation. Write out God's will in the following verses:

Ephesians 4:26 *In your anger do not sin.*

Matthew 18:15 (first part) *If your brother sins against you, go and show him his fault, just between the two of you.*

If only Christians would do the will of God, such problems would never develop.

Chapter 13 MINISTRY AND HOME

MINISTRY

How often as a pastor I have had church members come to me with the question, "What is my ministry? How can I find it?" This question arises from Paul's teaching on the Body of Christ in 1 Corinthians 12 and Romans 12:4-5. "I am a member of Christ's body, each part has a different function, so what is my function? What are my spiritual gifts? How can I discover my role?"

Firstly, would you please read carefully the whole of 1 Corinthians 12. In verse 1 Paul speaks of 'spiritual gifts'. In the NASB 'gifts' is in italics, which shows it is supplied by the translators and is not in the original Greek. His subject matter in this chapter is not just gifts but more generally 'spiritual things', the things which the Spirit does. What terms does he use to refer to these in verses 4-6?

1. *gifts* 2. *service* 3. *working*

In verses 7-10 is a list usually called the gifts of the Spirit. What words does Paul actually use to describe these in verse 7?

the manifestation of the Spirit

Paul is saying: "Here are some of the ways in which the Holy Spirit manifests Himself in and through each and every one of us." It is not a complete list; neither are these manifestations to be viewed as permanent endowments that we can operate at will. How do they come to us? (v. 11)

by the H/S giving them to us

How do we get these manifestations? Clearly we need to 'eagerly desire' them. They are only given to those willing to use them with the right motive of wanting to build up one another. Why are they given? (v.7)

for the common good

Housegroups are an excellent setting where we can reach out for and practise exercising these manifestations. There we can make mistakes and learn by them, and generally stimulate and encourage one another to be open to the Holy Spirit.

However, these are not just for meetings. The Spirit can manifest Himself in these ways in any of us, anywhere and at any time that He deems necessary. He may give words of knowledge, gifts of healing, discerning of spirits in all sorts of contexts. So we do need to cultivate a more open, expectant attitude to these things. For an example of this look at Acts 3:1-10.

Now although the Holy Spirit comes upon us in these ways to manifest Himself as He determines, we are not some passive ventriloquist's dummy on the Holy Spirit's knee. A great old hymn, "Channels only, blessed Master", has lent support to a rather unhelpful 'all of God, none of me' theology. In the prayer meeting before the service the deacons would pray for their minister: "Lord, we don't want to see our pastor this morning, but only Jesus." How tempting for the poor preacher to turn round and say, "OK then, we'll let Jesus preach the sermon this morning. I'll sit in the congregation." How can we see Jesus except as He is manifest in the lives of members of His body? This 'drainpipe' theology that tries to minimise any human contamination of the divine flowing through us is unrealistic and unbiblical. The Spirit manifests Himself in us, using our bodies, mouths, personalities, vocabulary and style, which is why Paul writes as he does in 1 Corinthians chapters 13 and 14. It has to be in love and under control. Write out 1 Corinthians 13:9:

For we know in part and we prophesy in part.

and 14:32:

The spirits of prophets are subject to the control of prophets.

The wonderful thing is that God uses us and manifests His power in us. But this only happens when we step out and speak what comes to mind, or reach out and pray for healing, or command a demon to go, or otherwise 'do what seems right'. Wonder of wonders, God actually works through us! Write out 2 Corinthians 4:7:

But we have this treasure in jars of clay to show that this all-surpassing power is from God and not from us.

We are just clay pots, but God loves to use us. I guess the more available we make ourselves to Him, through eager desire expressed in prayer, the more often He will use us. It's rather like the way some people have a favourite mug that they like to drink from! What does God see when He goes to the shelf to select a mug? "Here I am, all ready, Lord, please use me", or do we sit at the back getting all dusty, unused and unconcerned that He does not use us?

Special Gifts
Copy out 1 Peter 4:10:

Each one should use whatever gift he has received to serve others faithfully administering God's grace in its various forms.

and Romans 12:6:

We have different gifts according to the grace given us.

As with the latter part of 1 Corinthians 12, the writers are not speaking of the manifestations of the Spirit that are distributed as He wills according to the immediate needs, but of general areas of gifting and ability. Some of these, like prophecy, are giftings to specialise in one of the manifestations. Others seem to be much more general abilities, related to the way God has made us, involving our personalities and experience. Write down some of those listed in Romans 12:

serving, teaching, encouraging, contributing, leadership.

Compare 1 Timothy 3:2 and 2 Timothy 2:2.
What is one of the key gifts needed in a leader or a potential leader?

the gift of teaching.

How do we know if someone has it? Because they do it! You only have to watch them! They take hold of younger Christians and explain the truth to them and seek to develop their grasp of God's word. So too evangelists witness to people and get converts. Pastors get in amongst the needy and look after them. Servants are always there willing to do any job that is going. Contributors are always giving money away.

The whole emphasis of Paul's teaching in Romans 12:3-8 is, "If you can do something, then get on with it! God has given you the grace to do it, so just step out in faith and get stuck in." Or in the words of Ecclesiastes 9: 10 (first part), "Whatever your hand finds to do, *do it* ...." Life is too short to mess around thinking, "Could I be this, could I do that? If only I was an apostle or prophet!" If God has called us to be a prophet or a healer, He will make sure we become one. Our response and responsibility is to serve in whatever way we possibly can. We do not need 'recognition'. We do not need 'to be released into our ministry'. We just need to be ourselves, do what we can do and serve wherever we can serve. Proverbs 18:16 (NASB version) says, "A man's gift makes room for him." Copy it out from the NIV:

The gift opens the way for the giver.

While this may possibly refer to bribery, it is generally true that when we give a gift we open up a way that gains us approval and sometimes even recognition. Write out Jesus' words in the last part of Matthew 10:8:

The worker is worth his keep.

and the first sentence of Luke 6:38:

Give and it will be given to you.

Some have taken the approach, "Give yourself to God and He will use you"; others have countered that a more Biblical approach is, "Use the gifts that God has already freely bestowed on you and He will use you." However, Romans 12 combines both of these: "Give yourself to God, then get on and use your gifts and God will use you."

There is a place for trying something out. Can I do it? Is it my gift or not? Give it a go. Get some help, but if it does not really work, recognise that it is not really your thing and let someone else have a go (e.g. 1 Tim 3:10).

We really must deal with the wrong motivation that makes us seek recognition or looks for status. Our motivation must be to serve, whether we are recognised, acknowledged, promoted or not. We can gain an excellent standing and a great assurance, and even be ushered into the presence of the great, but only if we........serve well..................

....(see 1 Tim 3:13) because God exalts the humble, but the arrogant He deposes (Luke 1:52, James 4:16, 1 Peter 5:6).

"What is my ministry?"
"What can you do?"
"Well, I can .... and .... and .... and ...."

Good. So get on and do it and God will use you as you serve Him in these ways.

How I praise Thee, precious Saviour
That Thy love laid hold of me
Thou hast saved and cleansed and filled me
That I might Thy channel be.

Channels only, blessed Master
But with all Thy wondrous power
Flowing through us, Thou canst use us
Every day and every hour.

Mary E. Maxwell

HOME

Finally, we shall look at the question, "Where should I live?" I was 26, living at home with my parents and travelling some distance to the school where I was teaching. Things were rather sticky at the local Baptist church where I was a deacon. "It really is time for me to leave home, get into the property market, move nearer my job and find a church which is already charismatic." However, the very prospect of moving away made me realise my feelings for my sister's best friend. So, instead of moving away, Sandy and I got engaged. Six months later we were married and our wedding was the first thoroughly charismatic meeting the church had ever seen. We bought a flat locally and were very involved in supporting the pastor in spiritual renewal as people began to get baptised in the Spirit and use spiritual gifts in open worship. I later became co-pastor and now, ten years on at the time of writing, I lead the church. However, God has clearly indicated it is time for us to move on. Since starting this book on guidance, I have found myself having to respond very practically to its contents, not least regarding this very question, "Where should we live?"

Consider Adam, for whom at the dawn of time God planted a special garden to be his home. Consider also Abraham, who went out not knowing where he was going, to a land that God had promised him and his descendants in which to dwell. But home, to him, was a tent and, like the apostle Paul and the Lord Jesus Himself, he was 'of no fixed abode'. Write out Jesus' words in Matthew 8:20:

Foxes have holes and birds of the air have nests but the son of man has no where to lay his head.

When the children of Israel entered the Promised Land, each family was apportioned a piece of land as their inheritance and settled down to build on it and cultivate it. This was all part of God's purposes for His people. Consider the significance of Jerusalem, and of Bethlehem, which was Joseph's home town even though he had a carpentry business in Nazareth near Galilee. Thus Christ was called Jesus of Nazareth, from this inconsequential and despised northern town (probably in fulfilment of Psalm 22:6 and Isaiah 53:3), earning all the more contempt from His antagonists who did not know of His birth in Bethlehem, as prophesied by Micah (Matt 2:5-6) seven hundred years previously.

Clearly God does have an interest in geography, in the actual locations. But that interest is secondary to the people and events relating to those places. In considering "where", we need to ask the more pertinent questions, "Who is there?", "What is happening there?"

God calls each of us to be part of the action. It is totally foolish to move to some pleasant location in a nice house where there is absolutely nothing going on. If there is not a good church nearby, in which we can become thoroughly involved, we virtually commit spiritual suicide. So what if the job said you had to move, if it was the promotion you had been praying for for years, if you had always wanted to live in the country? We often face such materialistic temptations, and if we succumb, we can find ourselves wandering round in a spiritual wilderness for a whole wasted generation. Write out Jesus' words in Matt 6:33:

But seek first his Kingdom and his righteousness, and all these things will be given to you as well.

The boss may think you mad when you turn down the rise, the promotion, the all-expenses-paid relocation because of something about "a house-group" or "church commitments". You may even lose your job. But God is no man's debtor. If we sacrifice such materialistic gain and self-betterment for the Kingdom's sake, the Lord has ways of making it up to us.

The only exception to this principle of moving where we can be part of a lively church is if God is calling us out to pioneer; to go as lone lights in the midst of a dark area in order to see a group formed and a new church eventually spring up. We need the right gifts, firm faith, a proven record of success, a strong sense of God's initiative in this and lots of support from the local church who are sending us out, continuing with prayer, visits and other practical and spiritual help. We certainly need such pioneers today. But we dare not presume upon God's grace and 'do the Abraham bit' if we have not been given the vision of the stars of heaven.

Chapter 14 MAKING THE FINAL DECISION

God does not have a 'perfect plan' for our lives, like some blueprint design that we have to discover through prayer and on which we must pattern our lives. While each individual Christian's life features in God's eternal plan and infallible purpose for the universe, God constructs that plan in such a way as to take full account of all our decisions, Satan's demands, and our responses, both righteous and sinful. It is not a static, deterministic plan in which we are pawns on a chess board, neither does God subject His will to ours or change His mind depending on how we choose. Rather God unfolds His purposes in a process of dynamic interaction in which He remains absolutely sovereign while we each make our own decisions.

The process of guidance, by which we decide what to do with our lives, does not need to be a great hassle! An awesome realisation that we are caught up in God's purposes gives life security, wonder, comfort and a sense of meaning, direction and momentum. Mostly we have no difficulty making decisions because they almost make themselves. Either the scriptures give us specific instructions to be obeyed, or, by the wisdom of God's Spirit within us, we come to a conviction of the most appropriate decision to make.

When we do find ourselves in difficult situations, then we need to recognise that God is working in us to conform us more fully to His will; that is, to mould our character, teach us patience, trust, faithfulness and perseverance, to correct our sinful reactions and make us more like Jesus in holiness and godliness. Rather than trying to find ways to escape the situation, we need God's help to respond rightly and so to win through to the other side.

Every day of our lives we all have to make decisions. While most minor decisions are easy to make, we all have a natural tendency to avoid making more important ones. Each time we make one, we commit ourselves and take a definite pathway. It is much more comfortable to keep our options open. No one likes making such decisions. It can cause considerable stress and we all tend to avoid or postpone decision-making whenever we can. Christians do it just as much as non-Christians, but while non-Christians eventually face up to decisions that they have to make, we can continue to avoid responsibility by passing the buck – onto the Lord! He is all-knowing, all-wise. Let God make all the decisions, perfectly, and then all we have to do is 'discern the Lord's will', i.e. we do not make any decision ourselves, rather we try to discover the decision that God has already made. But this is not the way God works nor what the Bible teaches.

How easy it would be if we could get God to make all our decisions for us and tell us what to do at every step – but He does not and He will not! So we have to make our own choices. However, God gives us all we need to make those choices. He gives us the accumulated *wisdom* of the years of digging into His Word and of walking in His paths according to that Word. He gives us His own *Holy Spirit* to give us revelation and wisdom for each new situation we face. He gives us many *counsellors* with whom we can share and discuss, to whom we can submit our thoughts and ideas, and from whom we can gain essential information and insight.

Above all He gives us *prayer*, whereby we can clarify our thoughts by talking things through with the Lord, and through which we can pray our desires and plans into realities as we ask God to act on our behalf. In addition, from time to time He may unexpectedly break in with special instructions and fresh direction: dreams, visions, angels, audible voices, scripture verses, prophecies, warnings and strong impressions. This will usually confirm what we have already been considering, though occasionally, however, it will set us off on a whole new track – then we 'test the spirits' and check it out! If it is of God, it will always stand the test and be amply confirmed.

It is no use looking for the perfect partner, the dream house, the right church or the ideal job. They do not already exist. We are free to choose whom we want to marry; we pray for a suitable partner and as we grow in love and commitment together, he or she becomes our perfect partner. We are free to choose a house, so we look for a house or accommodation and pray for the features we would like. When God answers our prayers, we then work on it to fulfil our dreams. We are free to go to any local church, so we try one out and like what we see and hear. We know we could be happy here and submit to these leaders. This then becomes the right church for us at this time. We are free to choose a career, so we check out the job descriptions. "Yes, I could do this. It will stretch me, but will do me good and not conflict with my family and church interests", and we pray ourselves into a new job, ideal for now!

Disappointments? Sometimes, yes! But we can handle these by God's grace. "Many are the plans in a man's heart, but it is the Lord's purpose that prevails" (Proverbs 19:21), and we go on doing God's will by rejoicing and giving thanks and continuing in prayer.

Every decision, especially about marriage, home, church, ministry or job, will present us with difficulties, challenges and tests of faith. We've made our decision. Now we discover the problems. Regrets? No. It is futile to look back and say 'if only'. There may be lessons to learn, experience to acquire and wisdom to be gained. But what really matters is how we react and respond in those situations. Will we do the will of God by responding in righteousness and faith or will we sin? When we do God's will then our decisions are confirmed, we pass the test and get through the difficulties, coming out stronger, humbled and enriched.

We all make mistakes, says James. We do foolish things and make wrong decisions. Do we go 'down the tube'? No. We try and pick up the pieces, salvage whatever we can, go back to the starting point and choose the better way. We learn the lessons and give thanks to God for the grace and wisdom we have now received. It is all part of growing in the Lord. How blessed is the man who can say, "I blew it", without wallowing in self-pity, or struggling with pride; how blessed is the man who can graciously back down, rejoicing in total forgiveness, and confidently step out again without fear of failure. After all, this is essentially how we became Christians in the first place, isn't it? We came to God after a lifetime of wrong decisions and said, "I've blown it! I'm a sinner. I got it *all* wrong." We received God's grace and forgiveness, His love, acceptance and the power of His Spirit. We stepped out into a new life of fellowship with God with trust and confidence.

Did we become perfect? Did we gain instant utter sanctification? No.

We were just beginning on a path of discovery and growth into all that God wants us to become. But we can only keep growing if we maintain that same attitude of humble repentance, not thinking too highly of ourselves, but daily receiving fresh grace, forgiveness, acceptance, instruction and encouragement from God.

I guess if we walk in God's will, rejoicing, giving thanks and praying, daily being saved and sanctified, seeking always to be pleasing to God, we will not ever go far wrong. As Proverb 20:24 says, "A man's steps are directed by the Lord. How then can anyone understand his own way?" No, we will not understand all that happens to us, why certain events occur, or how we got from there to here. But we will know that God is with us and that as we make our plans He is at work in us in His own inscrutable way to will and to do His good purposes. Yes, we are safe and secure in His almighty hands.